MW01482121

They Call Me Ink

a collection of writing by New Zealand teenagers
selected by Tessa Duder
& James Norcliffe

edited by Glyn Strange

The 15th book in the Re-Draft series
sponsored by the School for Young Writers
and published by Clerestory Press
Christchurch

First published in 2016 by
CLERESTORY PRESS
P.O. Box 21120
Christchurch 8143
New Zealand

Email: clerestory@xtra.co.nz

ISBN 978-0-9922517-3-4
ISSN 1176-1806

A catalogue record for this book is available from
the National Library of New Zealand.

General series editor: Glyn Strange.
Cover illustrations by Jenny Cooper.
Book design and typesetting by Arnold Acres Design.
Printed by The Caxton Press, Christchurch.

Preface

My sister-in-law looks at the stack of A4 paper, nearly as high as a wine carton. "You don't have to read all that?" she asks, incredulously.

"Yep—and a lot several times," I smile.

"But that'd take weeks."

"Yes, but I do an hour here, two hours there. Sometimes in the car, waiting for grandson to finish choir practice. When there's absolutely nothing on TV, which is often."

She looks doubtful. "Doesn't it get a bit, well, tedious?"

I tell her emphatically, never. Far from tedious, it's thrilling. A privilege. You pick up the next story from the pile hoping this one is IT: the story or poem that grabs you from the first paragraphs, displays skill and daring with language, takes risks but still rings true. And finally satisfies, as a good short story or finely crafted poem should do. I've noticed that when I put down a really nice piece of work, I find myself giving a little grunt of pleasure.

With young writers there's a special delight in marvelling at fresh, even startling, insights into ancient themes and storylines. Now this author, you think, is going to go places; that one—well, needs to work at it. But every one of those stories has been thought about, drafted, edited and sent off by its author. That's the brave first step. So thank you, every single entrant, for stepping out, putting yourself and your story on the line.

This year James Norcliffe and I felt that the poetry entries were particularly strong. In a few cases we accepted two or even three by the same poet—well done! The prose pieces showed a terrific range of topics, with a few boldly tackling well-worn paths such as Gallipoli and memories of beloved grandparents. Some struck us as being more "writing exercises" than fully realised short stories; the potential was there but not explored. An instinct for knowing how far you might take an idea comes with experimenting, experience, more experimenting and reading widely.

Overall, a terrific collection for Re-Draft No 15 has emerged from the entries received. Congratulations to those whose work was chosen. To others, keep writing, keep trying, keep at it. Persistence is a key attribute of successful writers; you need about equal measures of perspiration and inspiration.

And please, please, always present your work with care and pride—this is just as true for a writing competition as it will be when ten years hence you're writing professional reports as an engineer or marketer or IT person or social worker. Or a job application.

Above all, the best practice for writing is … writing. Most writers I know have kept on going through rejection and disappointment with dogged determination till finally, an apprenticeship served, they have been rewarded.

Tessa Duder
Auckland, 2015

Contents

This edition of *Re-Draft* is dedicated to the memory of Christopher (Chris) Bates (1950–2015) in celebration of a life immersed in his own, and his students' creative writing.
An inspiration to many. May he rest in peace and rise in glory.

ZOË LEVACK

Awake

I have been up
            up
            up
all night for the past week
or so

It's like a slumber party, but it's just me
sitting in my bedroom and scratching away
at a sheet of paper, no makeovers or sugar highs
I play truth or dare with the pale face
giggling at me from the mirror

SOPHIE DONG

Untitled

some days
I sit there
yes, just there
beyond your peripheral vision

a mild headache
stomach ulcers don't develop
from just staring at unfinished essays

then I wonder
if it is worth it

how much
the world might change
if I would only get up

and write down
all the things I ever thought

ADELAIDE PERRY

Flags

Man sifts through A3 paper. Photocopies of copies. Giza pyramids, filled with a war-torn red. Dribbled blue. Salted with black ice, to add a buccaneering flair.

He, whose eyes are permanently glazed like Christmas ham, puffs his collector's cigar in endorsement, and leaves, leather shoes clicking on the wooden floorboards. The green gleam of money clashes with the bright white shine of the counter top.

Still, it feels nice in the pocket.

The paper arrives, droplets of rain still clutching the plastic cover. You shake it. You break their arms, they wet the carpet. Next to the heater, you unfurl the paper like the korus in options 1, 2, 6, 7, 34 and 36. Your finger traces the damp paper like the feathered ferns in flags 3, 4, 8, 11, 14, 15 and 28. All the same, you say, photocopies of copies of copied copies. You see one that looks like a new world-order pyramid of deli sandwiches. You don't notice the novel shade of red, or how methodically the particular shade of black complements the Arabian blue.

With the click of your pen you smear it with a large cross, in cheap ink.

You sigh, and grab the old flag. It shivers. You look at it, a copied cop-out for a copy cat country full of copies of cranky citizens.

It feels damp and heavy in your hand. You put it next to the fire, and you watch as the water droplets shrink away, escaping to dampen the carpet.

FREDDIE CORMACK-SMITH

The Alpha and the Omega

A single dark drop in a sea of non-existent clarity hunches in on itself in the centre of the beaker. Lonely, it breaks with a barely audible pop and spreads itself, rippling towards the inevitable cool glass.

Pinpricks of light glow momentarily, merge, and then fade back into the darkness. While oxygen and CO_2 are occupied in grappling for dominance, the contested dust particles implode and condense elsewhere. Matter and anti-matter circle each other like snakes—they strike, strangle, entwine for eternity. But eternity's end can be abrupt.

The scientist's back is turned, his hands occupied with the whistling kettle and precise spoonfuls of sugar and coffee granules. He fails to see his zit-stippled lab assistant grimace with distaste at the beaker and gingerly pour the liquid into the sink.

A universe swirls down the drain.

CHARLOTTE WILLIAMS

The Space Between Raindrops

The blank page is not white
but brown
with drought
bare
of inspiration

The mind is not black
but infinite blue sky

Thoughts
in the mind
are not fully formed words
but clouds
in the sky

Impatience is not an emotion
but the wind
that blows clouds away

Occasionally
the clouds will separate
and fall
of their own accord
dividing into small drops
inspired to grow bigger

The drops are not transparent
but iridescent
and when they fall
the blank page
is no more

Welcome to fanfiction.net

Have you ever finished that movie, book, or TV show your friends were dying to let you watch, and just thought: wouldn't it be nice if the story went differently? Have you ever thought you had a better idea for the plot of your favourite book? Or ever imagined the ensuing hilarity of your favourite characters spending a day in your school?

If any of the above applies to you, and you want to take your fandom the next step further, I have just the solution. There is a way to keep your favourite characters alive. If you're an avid fan or aspiring author, then you're bound to discover one of the internet's biggest centres of Writer's Heaven and Hell combined.

I welcome you, dear reader, to fanfiction.net. As an old-time member of the site, let me be the first to welcome you through the doors. Before, it seemed my enthusiasm for stories and shows could only take me as far as squealing over fan-made art and new releases. Then, one fateful day, I happened to click onto one published fanfic… and the world opened. I had stepped into the world's largest fanfiction archive, where fanfic writers and readers around the globe gather to share their passion.

Why is it dubbed Writer's Heaven and Hell combined, you ask? Well, when there aren't any English teachers to scrutinize published pieces, anything can happen. An hour inside, browsing around, and you'll get your fair share of things like Rabid Fangirl, Brutally Honest Reviewers and Mutant Plot Bunnies, alongside amazingly creative spin-offs and politely supportive comments. We tread with caution here; one can never know if the next story is utterly engrossing or well-that's-enough-time-on-the-internet-for-me material. But don't let that scare you, budding authors. I have ventured through this site long enough to find three Fanfiction Commandments that guarantee safe travel.

> One: Thou shalt be knowledgeable of a fandom's own language before proceeding. In other words, make sure you understand terms like AU, Canon, Angst, OTP, and the context to use "Fluff" and "Drabble" as you rate and label your pieces. Otherwise you'll end up clicking on a harmless looking story and find yourself traumatised for life. Authors should warn you beforehand if they've suddenly decided to switch the gender of the main character.

> Two: Thou shalt not be excused terrible grammar just because it is not English class. You'll be doing yourself a favour when you press that spell-check button. Really.

> Three: Thou shalt strive to keep thy characters as realistic to the canon story as possible in thy spin-offs. *Exempli gratia*: Samwise Gamgee is a loyal, quiet hobbit, not an alcoholic deadbeat father. Fred and George Weasley are class clowns, not competitive Harvard entrants. See what I mean? If a character knows nothing about fighting, do not make them army commanders. In the world of fanfiction, wedding bands last only as long as the original author's book

does, but that doesn't mean you should completely change what truly defines the characters you love. Enhancing a story does not mean destroying every semblance of the original.

And please, please, for the love of all those who read, DO NOT create annoyingly perfect characters. There is a reason why a flying, telepathic, telekinetic, invisible Jedi who can get any girl he wants because he's also drop-dead gorgeous AND can defeat the biggest, meanest bad guy in the space of one paragraph, doesn't exist in the actual story. Mary-Sues, or Gary-Stus, they call them. Steer clear of these infamous nuisances or kiss goodbye any hope of a positive review.

The bottom line is this: writing has rules, and if you're going to make your work available publicly, you should make an effort not to disappoint.

That being said, if I haven't scared you away already, fanfiction.net will be your safe haven when you enter with literary flair and a generous dusting of common sense. The great part about joining it is that limits for story ideas do not exist here. If you have a prose piece detailing a day with your favourite character selling pizza at Domino's, no one is stopping you. Dream, write, publish, and be pleasantly surprised with the knowledge that there are people out there just as enthusiastic about your fandoms as you are.

And so, fellow fans, budding authors, I welcome you. I welcome you to fanfiction.net, where imagination runs wild and where finishing a book doesn't mean finishing the story.

ERIN DONOHUE

Write

Write poems that are battle cries
and body armour.

Write poems that breathe fire
or glow in the dark.

Write poems that scream from rooftops,
poems that shatter silence.

Write poems that burn holes in your pockets
when you try to keep them
to yourself.

Take-off is Optional, Landing is Mandatory

"LET'S GO LET'S GO LET'S GO! MOVE IT, PEOPLE!"

Honestly, trying to get Nepthys and Drew to *move* when we're in mortal danger is too much to ask. You'd think the multitude of bullets and explosions everywhere would tell them *Oh, we're in danger. We should probably go, like, RIGHT NOW*—but no. No, they stand there and gawk at the small army coming to kill us. So I get to yell and scream at them to *just bloody move*, and all but shove them onto the plane. Okay, that's a lie. I *did* actually shove them onto the plane. Who knew it was possible to trip *up* stairs, 'cause apparently Nep can. The poor sods—this is Nepthys and Drew, mind you—were so overwhelmed by all the craziness of this dimension that they could barely function, and it was all perfectly normal to me. I'm still pissed that those private militia types shot up my plane, though. Once holes started appearing in my *pressure-sensitive*, beautifully painted and damn expensive jet, I had had enough.

"ALL RIGHT THEN! YOU TOSSERS WANT IT, COME AND GET IT! Drew, get this idiot on the plane, lock the doors and keep them that way. I'll phase in when I'm finished with these pricks."

That apparently was enough to snap Drew out of his stupor. "Uh, Maya? They have *guns*. And a freaking *tank*!"

(Side note: Drew and I each have multiple names, being multi-dimensional beings and all, so we just use whichever ones feel comfortable at the time. I'm normally Zeke or Maya, he's normally Drew or Philip).

"So? When has that stopped me? And they shot. My bloody. Plane. This thing cost me a couple of million dollars. *And* it was due to be bullet-proofed next week! With everything that's been going on, it's about time I let off a little steam, don't you think?"

"I'm sorry, did you say a *couple of million* dollars?!"

"That's nothing in this world, Drew. And we really don't have time for this. NOW MOVE!"

I'm just going to take a moment to describe the beauty of the scene. Imagine one of the many small airports not far from Chicago, Illinois, with 100 or so armed security types and a small tank on the tarmac. (Where in the hell did they get a tank! And how did they get it onto the tarmac?) Add a large-ish private jet type thing—I think it was a small Boeing—to the chaos, with Drew standing in the doorway, holding a barely conscious Nepthys by the scruff, like a cat, and bullets sinking through the metal all around them. I'm at the bottom of the stairs, shoving the boys up them and yelling in multiple languages, with bullets stopping about a foot from my body and falling to the ground. Not to mention the manic glint in my pitch black eyes or the essentially evil grin beginning to show. A truly b-e-a-utiful moment, because it's still the last sane one left before all hell broke loose.

**** About 5 seconds later ****

I just love those days when the world all goes to hell. Truly, I do. They give me an excuse to break things and generally be the devil incarnate. Trying to keep up with the wanton destruction is another thing, however. What Drew calls the "dark dancer'—which is essentially me turned homicidal, an overpowered succubus. Apparently I'm attractive in some weird, dangerous way when I'm like that. I don't see it, personally—has a habit of killing everyone and everything it can. In this case, the small army marching up the tarmac. Poor sods. Flowing from one dimension to another has steadily become easier over the years, so jumping between them to move from one spot to another without being seen is nothing. The wisps of smoke that result from dimension-hopping can be rather poisonous to most species, so it's an added bonus that I can control that too. Well, it's more like I control the anti-matter particles in between the poisonous matter and nudge it in the right direction. Anyway, it's time for a fight scene!

An ethereal calm can be found in the noise of battle. The approaching militia were basically silent as I stood between them and my prizes. (Note to self: I am extremely possessive when I go dark.) The bullets they were firing at us weren't so silent as they ricocheted off everything and even took down a few of their own men. As I stepped towards them, the exposure of the scene began to increase, amplifying the light and the dark to ridiculous levels (observers have told me that this is just *my* sight changing, and my eyes turn pitch-black). I walked forward slowly, graceful and lithe as a panther. Everything about me had gone dark; my hair was rippling out behind me like black flames. Even my clothes were laced with dancing shadows, the poisonous smoke common to the gap between dimensions, hanging around me in tendrils. I began to shimmer like a phantom, my hold on the dimensions slipping out of reach. Every step I took would propel me several metres forward as I walked through multiple realms at once, appearing and disappearing in different places. Awareness of the space between everything—people, mechanical parts, matter, *atoms*—began to seep into my consciousness, providing *so many* ways to do things. A flick of my thoughts and I could destroy so much. But I settled for the idiots on the tarmac. The bullets began to curve as they flew towards me, creating a miniature whirlwind of metal and smoke. The inter-dimensional force propelling me forward makes for a great weapon, and I sent men flying with no more than a small shove.

It's normally about now that Drew will interrupt with a Star Wars joke, saying, "the Force is strong in this one" or something. IT'S A COMPLETELY DIFFERENT FORCE! The one that Drew and I experience is the universe trying to say No, you're not supposed to be in that dimension. Not that one, either. NO, NOT THERE! GET BACK HERE RIGHT NOW, YOU INTER-DIMENSIONAL TRUANT! Oh, fine, go that way then! See if I care. … Well actually, I do. COME BACK! It's like a massive invisible tug-o-war between me and the universe. I usually win, though. So when the universe gives up, the force rebounds on me and gives me a little extra oomph. Star Wars force is the life force of their universe. Massive difference.

You know, now that I think about it, I've never been great at re-telling fight scenes. There's so much going on at once that if I detailed every single thing that happened it'd be a book all by itself. Plus my tendency to ramble and/or be interrupted by the others makes things stupidly long. So I'm just going to paraphrase.

I went dark really quickly, and became seriously overpowered when compared to you lot. Examples of this include super-running, super-punching, appearing and disappearing at will, poisonous smoke I can control with my mind, gravity defying jumps ... *aaand* the general bad-assery that comes with being an inter-dimensional being that's not supposed to exist. The smoke is and most likely always will be my main weapon, though. I can use it in so many ways. Very little actually hit me thanks to my little whirlwind, and there weren't any massive explosions or anything (much to my disappointment: I love explosions). Though one of my favourite moments was when one of the guys I super-punched went flying and was skewered on the barrel of the tank's main gun. He-he-he.

I made quick work of the private militia, surprisingly without all that much blood. Most of them just ended up looking unconscious, with limbs bent at strange angles or in funny places. Not to mention they themselves were in funny places. There was the guy skewered on the tank barrel, of course, but I also saw a few guys way up over on the hangar roofs, and some draped over nearby planes. I could hear distant screaming, so I'll assume that a few made it to the terminal. Then again, human bodies have never been the most aerodynamic, so let's not jump to conclusions. I had left one or two alive, just to pass on the message, and I could see them scrambling off in the distance. Deciding that was my cue, I stepped back into the inter-realm between worlds and wandered over to see Drew.

**** Drew's POV, a minute or so later****

I really hate it when Zeke decides to mess with me. She sees it as fun, but I just loathe those moments when she's ready to destroy the universe. Not to mention she normally takes it out on me. The most I get is a few seconds' warning when I can feel the dark matter shifting too much to be normal. This time, however, Zeke was feeling more mischievous than death-hungry. We both have the slight whispers of the inter-realm constantly running through our minds, but she likes to mess with the volume controls every now and then. I mean, its useful if we're trying to find each other, because we can just play hot and cold, as it were. But when you're dealing with a screaming scribe in a locked plane cabin and every sound begins to screech like a high C, and you know exactly who's doing it, you tend to get just a little bit pissed. And here everyone is saying that I'm the calm one. Have you tried actually living with Zeke? That does not make for a calm or tolerant person.

"Maya, I swear to whatever bloody gods there are, if you don't quit it right now ..."

Thankfully she chose that moment to pop back into reality. Well, she popped in a good two metres above the floor, so she landed straight on top of me.

"Oof! Did you really have to do that, Zeke? In the grand scheme of the universe, was that really all that necessary for our survival?"

"Oh, come on Drew, it's not that bad. And to answer your question: yes, yes it was."

An exasperated sigh was all I could muster as I watched her bounce into the cockpit. She gets so chipper after completely losing her mind that it's nauseating. Although watching Zeke at the controls of a plane never ceases to terrify me. Even more so when I can still see the shreds of her dark homicidal nature in her eyes. It's times like these I just pray to whatever deities there are that we'll live to see another day. And if that doesn't work, I stall for time.

"What exactly are you planning to do, Maya? It's not like we can just take off and leave.

There's still a tank in the middle of the runway, in case you haven't noticed."

"TAKING OFF IS OPTIONAL! IT'S ONLY LANDING THAT'S MANDATORY!".

Comments like these really just define Zeke and her particular brand of crazy. Only do what's required, no more, no less. And try not to die. Again.

"WHAT KIND OF LOGIC IS THAT? AND WHY ARE WE YELLING?"

"IT'S CALLED PHYSICS! AND BECAUSE THERE'S MORE OF THOSE IDIOTS COMING UP BEHIND US! NOW BUCKLE UP AND PRAY THIS THING CAN TAKE ON A TANK!"

"WHAT?!"

It's this next moment that I will forever be thankful for. Zeke told me later that her plan was to use the sloped front of the tank like a ramp and drive straight over it. Thankfully that wasn't necessary, owing to an unexpected guest. Zeke's theory is that the stranger wanted to hijack our plane for nefarious purposes. Mine is that she was simply evading those official-types, like the rest of us, and had the same idea we did: get in the air, get away. The visitor never said anything, so I guess we'll never know. She did, however, proceed to tap me on the shoulder whilst I was arguing with Zeke, and point a rather sharp knife at my throat. It wasn't the first time this had happened so I only freaked out in my head.

Nepthys, however, chose this exact moment to regain consciousness and started screaming. "EZEKIAS! THERE'S A NINJA PERSON POINTING A KNIFE AT DREW!"

Zeke didn't buy it. Never does. "Will you stop with the idiocy for two minutes, Nep? That's all I'm asking for: two minutes! Drew, gag him please."

At this point the owner of the knife, obviously getting impatient, waved at me to talk.

"Kinda can't do that, Maya. There actually is a ninja-looking person pointing a knife at my throat."

"Oh, for crying out loud! Why can't we just have a remotely normal day for once?"

Because we're not human, that's why. We're made of dark matter, and that attracts trouble.

Speaking of trouble, the said ninja person let go of me for all of two seconds to throw some sort of weight at Nepthys' head, because Nep hadn't stopped screaming. That shut him up real quick. And then she was back, knife and all, nudging me back towards the door and waving in the general direction of Zeke. I guess she wasn't in a talkative mood.

"Maya, can you come in here please? I would like to keep my throat intact and this knife is really sharp."

Thank the gods that Zeke's not completely crazy. All you gotta do is threaten someone she cares about and you're *gone*. Although, seeing as she's my girl, I suppose I do get special priority. She phased in, right in front of me.

"Get. Away. From. Him. NOW."

As the ninja was behind me, all I felt/heard was a brief hiss, her shaking her head, and the knife digging into my throat some more.

"He's *mine*, you can't have him. Now Let. Him. Go."

I do love it when Zeke gets possessive.

"She's right, you know, I'm hers. And she's rather possessive of her toys, so I would probably just–"

The hissing was back, slithering out right next to my ear. Not a pleasant experience. Although this time it sounded almost like *laughing*, hitching and stuttering as though this was the funniest thing in the world. And then it started sounding like a voice. Zeke and I worked out later that we automatically translated it.

You think I want this pathetic man-child as a mate? Please. What I want is to get off this plane. What I want is to get away from you lot. My team is bad enough, but you? Forget it.

The knife was too close to risk talking, so I just let Zeke handle it for once.

"Um … well, there's currently another small army coming up the tarmac, so it might not be the best idea if we let you off right now. We just need to–"

I already have reinforcements on their way. They'll deal with it. Until then its probably best if we stay inside.

"Uh huh. I'm assuming that's what the low humming is?"

Yes.

"Mind if I take a look?"

Be my guest.

I still can't listen to that bloody song, because Zeke started humming it after our new friend said that. AND THE NINJA JOINED IN! Try imagining a snake singing. It's creepy!

Be our guest, be our guest, put our service to the test! Tie your napkin round your neck, cherie, and we'll provide the rest!

****Zeke's POV****

I have to admit, I was mildly impressed. This ninja managed to sneak onto my plane, shut Nepthys up and threaten my boyfriend without me realising. And she knew her classic movies! Damn. SLIGHT girl crush. Moving on!

After that rather brief confrontation, as stated before, I was mildly impressed. Although when I opened the cabin door and leaned outside, I wasn't expecting what was a rather fortified jeep gunning it up the tarmac behind the new batch of idiots. There was also a girl leaning out the window with a bazooka. *Wait a sec. A bazooka?*

"BAZOOKA! HIT THE FLOOR!"

I tackled Drew across the small room and landed on Nepthys, instinctively reaching for them both on an atomic level. Mute, dark and grouchy just stood there looking a) like I was crazy and b) bored, as if she had seen it all before. Just as I was about to scream at her to brace, get down, or something, the rocket hit something.

WHOOM!

We didn't die. We didn't even get badly injured. The shock wave threw us around, but nothing we couldn't handle.

"I'm assuming that was your reinforcements?"

Most likely.

"Most likely? What kind of answer is that?"

My answer. Care to step outside?

"Not really. May as well, though."

Outside was total carnage. Everything was … well, there are no polite words for it, to be honest. Surprisingly, my plane was fine. Actually, it looked brand spanking new. No bullet holes or anything. *What the hell? Who in the thousand realms touched up my plane?* I walked around the tail and found the kid that had the bazooka applying a fresh lick of paint to the side, with two taller girls playing chicken with the propeller nearby. They looked like identical twins, now that I think about it.

"Oi! Get your grubby mitts off my plane! This thing is expensive!"

The twins just looked at me like I was a nutter and resumed spinning the propeller. The smaller girl dropped her paintbrush and pulled out an axe—*a freaking tomahawk*—faster than I could blink.

"You wanna go, mate? After we just saved your sorry asses, and patched up your plane, you wanna try your luck?"

"Sure, I can go another round. But one to three ain't fair to you guys."

"Girlie, you don't even know the half of it. You know, I've been wanting to get a plane lately, and I think yours just might make the cut."

"Oh, hell no! Kid, back the hell off. Unless you wanna spend the short period that'll be the rest of your life in the crushing abyss between worlds."

"Give a man a fire, and he'll be warm for a day. Set a man on fire, and he'll be warm for the rest of his life. I've got matches and gasoline, if you want me to prove that theory."

ENOUGH! Alex, this is all your fault, so you don't get to start ANYTHING right now!

I had completely forgotten that the ninja had walked round with me.

The kid (Alex, did she say?) flinched and started waving her hands, lunatic fashion. And gibbering in Latin, I think. Ninja just nodded and waved at the twins, who stopped spinning the propeller (thank the gods, 'cause those things are hard to fix, expensive too) and walked back to the jeep. Doors slammed shut, the engine revved, and in a heartbeat they were half way down the tarmac.

As I turned to watch them leave Drew waltzed on over with Nepthys in a fireman's carry over his shoulder.

"Um … do I want to know what happened?"

"I don't even know, Drew. I don't even know."

CIAN SUTHERLAND

The Wandering Colossus

During my travels I encountered a small black book proclaiming to contain the 221 unused ideas of H. P. Lovecraft. Detailed within are scraps, thoughts begging to be acted on. And so I take it upon myself to try, as best I can, to fulfill their wish and create prose from them. Here is idea number 21, as it was found:

21. A very ancient colossus in a very ancient desert. Face gone—no man hath seen it.

A very ancient colossus roams a very ancient desert, an infinite expanse of mounded sand eroded by harsh winds that sweep themselves up into abrasive storms. Every footstep shakes the world, the heart of the desert trembling as the colossus makes its equally infinite traversal. Its feet sink into the ground as it walks, leaving massive impressions step by step, only to have them covered by sand that flows and shifts in synchronicity with its movements. Each heavy impact sends up a cascade of sand that lets itself be stolen by the howling winds, blustering backwards to lay flat and heap over the tracks the colossus would leave behind: a constant erasure of the passing of the colossus, and of its existence.

A lonely soul burdening a journey with neither a beginning nor an end. Just a middle. An endless middle. A bipedal beast of incomprehensible size, hard rock with a soft, beating heart that thrums in time with the heart of the desert. It is the only living being inhabiting the arid expanse, unless one counts the moss and vine that adorn its body and intertwine with its mineral joints. Almost as if they hold all the limbs together.

But the most arresting of its features is not its magnificent size, or its shape, or its sonorous groans which echo and resonate despite the frequent winds. No, most noticeable is its face, a face consumed by grating sand and wind, abraded by what has already been an infinity. Worn away by time, until all that now remains is a smooth, blank stone slate.

No mortal eyes had ever been laid upon the face of the colossus as it once was, in the time before time when it was not condemned to a purgatorial eternity of endlessly traversing the desert. No mind exists to recall with trembling, frightened awe and wonderment the planes and angles of its sculpted physiognomy. Nothing has or will ever be left that could attest to its existence at all.

H.P. Lovecraft (1890–1937), fantasy fiction author

The Music Machines

When the second-officer opened the door, it felt like rising from under water. A surge of heavy sound broke full across his chest. It rattled his jaw bones and sent the metal deck beneath his feet into a low, warm hum. Unperturbed, he walked across the room, placed the tray of food down on a table, and cast his eyes over at the source.

The girl waltzed beneath a cove of computers. They curved over and around her like a wave on the brink of breaking. Wide-screen monitors, shingled end to end, were flickering with brief strains of musical staves that wound on and on, in an endless spaghetti tangle, and the girl was reading them. Her eyes were blazing in severest concentration on the screen, but at the same time she was dancing, twirling wrists, stamping feet, swirling body.

The officer quickly realised that she was the one making the music. Her hands sculpted the orchestra with intricate delicacy, bending it and kneading it and moulding it like clay: her palms rendering the string section smooth and deft, flicks of her elbows and hips instructing the brass, her fingers rippling the individual notes of piano and harp. The music machine and the girl were inseparable, a single entity fluttering about the raised platform with a gossamer-like voice.

But with sudden energy she struck violently forward—she stomped, and a thundering percussion roared across the chamber. The tubas and the standing basses blared furiously, violins and violas and cellos screamed down and up and down, while the wind section fluttered above it all with uneasy meekness. Throwing her arms about her head, she thumped about the stage, bending low with one sweeping hand to draw out the dark, rich, powerful voice of the bass clef, and twisting with the other hand in the agonies of higher notes. She pranced, she stalked, and the music mimicked her anger.

Then with a light-hearted hop she went swinging down into a jazzy tumble, her feet nimbly picking out the deep, rich rocking of the bass notes. With a twirling of her arms and wrists, she scurried up and down the brassy scales, letting the saxophone warble warmly to itself while the drums hissed and fizzled away in a corner. The music was a live thing, and she twisted with it, mingling hands and mingling glances.

And into a fury she ran, dancing victoriously as the music rampaged around her. A triumph of trumpets, plethora of pipes, fluster of flutes, and strident tattoo of a swift-tapping drum were all swept up in a dizzying whirlwind of climactic sound; booming under her toes and shrieking happily round her wrists and swelling up, up into an enormous bulging on-the-brink-of-crescendo. She raced, she skipped, she spun, she danced. And with a magnificent, heart-bursting leap she and the music soared to their very zenith—limbs arching, pulses blooming, bursting, curving, curling over—spiralling up and up and up and up and crashing down into a beautiful, crouching silence.

She tumbled off the platform like a bundle limp with exhaustion but radiating with triumph.

"I did it!" she laughed as he moved to lift her off the floor. An enormous grin split her face. "Did you see me? Did you hear it all? I got it to work, Simm! I finally got it to work!"

"I saw," he said placidly, lifting her weight onto his arm and gently steering her over to where he'd placed the meal.

13

"Ha-haa! Isn't it the coolest thing ever? I knew it would work!"

"Yes, Jackie." Continuing in that cool, even way of his, he drew the tray closer and placed it on her lap. "Now it's time to eat. They told me you hadn't taken in a meal in over twenty-four hours."

She gave a long, drawn out sigh of satisfaction. "That long, huh? That long? I know how long. I've *always* wanted to build that machine."

"Eat," he repeated, and she started on a corner of bread. Her eyes, still shining like sunlight in a bubbling spring, were fixed on the massive machine, now hunched over like an old man bending to embrace a child, trailing whiskers of wires, circuit-boards, and diodes.

He sat down on the bed above her and sent his inky gaze in the same direction.

"Back home, my family could never afford for me to play music," she told him. He remained silent, but she could hear him listening. "There was all the cost of buying and then maintaining the instrument. And, of course, decent tuition involves forking out a fair bit as well. It's not cheap. I wanted it more than anything in the world; even when I went crazy with begging, they always said no. They tried to comfort me by saying I would've got sick of it and given up anyway, so there wasn't any point in wasting money."

Jackie raised her chin proudly. "I knew it wasn't a waste. My school taught music theory for free, at least, so I studied that instead. Eight solid years. And now look," she raised her hands to the machine and laughed, "I am a Maestro!"

He glanced at her with dark, expressionless eyes. She had forgotten to eat again, so he pushed a bunch of grapes into her palms. "From the lab garden."

"Fresh fruit!" She bit luxuriously into one. "Genetically sweetened?"

"I should say so."

"Mmm. Not as good as the red grapes our neighbour had. If you got them at just the right time, you could suck the fruit right out of the skin and have only the jelly sweetness all rolling around in your mouth. You ever eaten grapes like that, Simm?"

"No."

Momentarily distracted, Jackie bounced her teeth off the grape skin, realising for the first time that she'd never seen the second-officer eat before. For a moment it seemed a strangely necessary thing. But fixing her eyes on the machine, her mind re-boarded her train of thought.

"I used to be so jealous of my friends back then, you know." She glanced up at his motionless figure and smiled. "They were all so brilliant and smart and talented. *They* could all play violas and … oboes, whatever. That was 'cos they were from such well-to-do families. I used to cry 'cos I wanted to be able to speak fluent French and Spanish and Italian just like them. But look at me! I read music like you'd read a book. I can teach a machine how to sing." She rested her arms on her knees, sighing to herself with a smile. "And so what?"

Not taking his eyes from the machine, he asked, "What do you mean, 'so what'?"

Jackie scratched the side of her face and shrugged. "You think it was worth working on?"

"Yeah, I enjoy it. It shows your talent."

Jackie chuckled again, more to herself. "Y'know Simm, I used to cry a lot when I was younger. I cried because I was never *good* at anything, not in the way other people talk about it, and definitely not how my friends were." She took three grapes and chewed on them slowly. "Once, at my neighbour's house, I was wallowing in self-pity over it, and she turned around and snapped, 'So what? So what? You're kind. You're the most caring person I know. You're good at THAT.' "

Laughing, Jackie tossed a green grape in the air, missed it, and it fell and split on the cold metal floor. "It was funny 'cos I felt like she was saying I was good at being human. Like that was my talent."

"Perhaps it is."

"Then isn't it everyone's? It's like, if you're good at being human, it's being who you're supposed to be."

Simm turned his head and stared intently at her. "Who are we supposed to be?"

"Human."

"That begs the question of what it means to be human," he answered, turning his head away again.

"I bet there's a ton of ink spilled on that subject. Everyone thinks they know the answer best. Even me."

"Not everyone demands their infallible opinion on it, though."

"But you know what I mean, Simm. Just the way a person behaves..."

"...expresses what they unconsciously believe a human should be," he finished coolly. "I understand. That said, everybody can live their lives being what they believe a human should be. The problem occurs when people hold opposing views, and one tries to push their view on another."

"No human has the right to cage another and say they're wrong. That's treating them like animals."

"Hence," Simm replied, "your theory follows the line that everybody can live in an isolation of their own humanity. No one has the right to condemn another, and no one shall."

In the silence that followed, his black eyes didn't look at her, but stayed fixed on the machine.

"Simm, what sort of crap is that?" Jackie laughed. "Oh, man, that's not what I meant. What it means to be human can't be decided by any one human, simply because they don't hold any authority over anyone else. Not even themselves." She grinned and popped another grape in her mouth. "So tell me, Simm, who tells us who we are?"

He looked down at her, and for the first time Jackie could see the faint shine of something deep in his fathomless eyes.

"No one."

She snorted. "It's like saying music is nothing but vibrations."

His eyes remained pinned to her face, searching for the meaning of her words.

She rolled her eyes. "C'mon. Music is not only vibrations. Music has tune, tone, rhythm, beauty, ugliness, warmth and coldness. It's dynamic. It has life. You're not deaf, Simm. Didn't you hear anything?"

When he didn't answer, she swallowed her mouthful and asked, "What do you think?"

"It does not mean anything to be human, Jackie."

She turned, tossed the last grape into her mouth, and said, "Then why are we hungry for it?"

ESTHER HISCOCK

If You Ask Me Why

My mother never played classical music to me when I was younger. No Mozart while I was in the womb. No tuneful childcare playgroups. So when, at age 12, I had an epiphany and decided to learn the violin, there were some raised eyebrows! If you ask me why the violin… to be honest I had no idea. A friend, Emily, played exceedingly well and her musically exuberant mother, who had background classical playing 24/7, suggested that I be given the gift of learning by the Suzuki method. It is considered by those within the movement to be one of the best methods around! It develops the ear by listening to a CD with graded pieces played well. Memory is trained as each piece is mastered and retained. The time taken to achieve this is as varied as each individual. Finally, confidence at performing is secured as students get frequent opportunities to play, together and solo, to an audience of supportive parents and teachers who are able to endure a cacophony of sounds and still respond with applause. My mother had no idea what it all meant, but she expectantly signed me up, then shifted herself to a shadowy corner in the auditorium to practise the rhythmic coming together of her palms!

Thanks for the gift, Mum.

Now before I go on I would like to explain some things about the Suzuki method:
1. You should be aged zero when you start.
2. It helps to be a child prodigy.
3. It could be advantageous to be of Asian descent or have ancient, melodious parents.

None of the above applied to me. My parents are hopelessly tone deaf and my father struggles to clap in time. My uncle does play the bagpipes, but I don't think that counts towards musicality. With Suzuki, you start with *Twinkle Twinkle Little Star*. I never knew it could be played so many different ways! About half way through Book One, I really wanted to quit. Memorization was arduous, the pace was tedious and those seven-year-old Mozart midgets played better than I could. Oh the shame. I, an oversized giant like Gulliver among the Lilliputians. Why had I started so late? I really wanted to have a Bogan-like bash at drums. Mum was mean. She wouldn't let me discontinue my studies, but said I could add drums. MUM became an acronym for mean, unreasonable and merciless.

Thanks for making me stick at it, Meany.

Just when things looked really bleak and inspiration was desperately needed, I accidentally stumbled across Lindsey Stirling, who was marketing herself on YouTube with fresh and exciting videos. Suddenly the violin had a new look: it was electric, pounding out dubstep as hip as glittery shoes! There was life beyond the music stand and, being so tall, I could see it! I knew I could do this. Lindsey not only plays and dances energetically with fantastic costumes reflecting the story of her music, she also presents awesome collaborations with other musicians. Amazingly, she sells her sheet music. Call it pearls before swine, I have bought some which I endeavour to play! Personally, I don't know how she frolics about

16

while playing because I have tried and risked doing serious bodily harm to myself, my violin and any onlookers. It is fantastic to know you can appreciate and not need to emulate. At a time when I was harmonising with Handel, beating it out with Bach and swinging it with Seitz, her music propelled me into the modern age. It thrust me from a quiet concert chamber into a throbbing mosh pit, and you don't see many seven-year-olds there.

Thanks Lindsey for the inspiration!

The violin, as an instrument, is marvellous. It is light and portable. It requires an intelligent player, if I do say so myself, for the violin has no fret-board for ease of note location. You have to listen to find the right sound. Instruments with frets are for wimps; the violin is not for the faint of heart. The violin can be plucked, bowed, slapped or tickled to produce a range of sounds, much like my brother really, but less retaliatory! No translation is needed when it speaks, for it commands attention. The looks of the violin are endless and I aspire to have a wardrobe of them to complement every costume. There are colourful ones, electric skeletal, diamond studded, five-string violins and the classic wooden finish, to name but a few. As a starving artist, I have the latter. It is so diverse that even its sturdy case has multiple uses. It has been famed as a discreet carry-all for gangsters' guns and is also great for busking to collect those showers of coins.

Thanks generous public!

This fabulous instrument has taught me to persevere through tough times, knowing I'll get my rest at the end of the bar. I know I am living proof that age or starting late isn't an issue. Sometimes it is an advantage. It is blatantly obvious that we all play at different levels and move at different speeds, so why sweat the small stuff? Don't hide behind excuses, just start! There are always rewards for work and effort made. I have learnt to appreciate the people above me, encourage the ones below me, and always strive for a new personal best.

Finally, I have to say that music is a most precious gift. It is a universal language that everyone can understand. If more people spoke it, although it is not an easy one to learn, there would be fewer arguments! If you ask me now why I play violin—I've just told you.

Thanks, audience!

Why Not

My brother asks me why I photograph the sky. He asks to see the picture, and I hand him my phone.

"Why?" he says, because when he looks back up at the horizon all he sees is a Tuesday morning. He doesn't see how fast the sun has risen behind the clouds. He doesn't see the way the cotton layers have peeled away to reveal spindles of light straining to brush the grass.

I'm so busy contemplating the sky that I almost forget his question. I glance at the sunrise on my phone before I put it back in my pocket. I'm not sure how to answer him.

I could say how this sunrise, this Tuesday morning, will never be seen again by any human being, ever. It'll spiral up and fly away with each passing minute. Lost to the wind, unless someone sticks out a hand to catch it, clutches it tight so that even if it's been torn and crumpled it can't slip away.

I could tell him about the way the houses wink at me in the orange light. About the sun-soaked grass, their tiny blades dancing in their sparkling dew dresses. I'd point at the bare tree branches stretching up to reach the sky. I'd tell him that this Tuesday morning is sitting in my pocket now, safe from time.

He'd probably laugh at me, tell me to stop worrying about taking photographs of everything. "Live in the moment." And I'd laugh right back at him. When I'm old, when my face is tissue paper tearing with every smile, I won't have to grasp frantically at my memories as they fall away like sand in an hourglass. They'll be safe, stored in gilded crystal frames on my desk instead of the fragile murk in my mind. Tuesday morning, the single moment of the sun being carried up over the hills by purple clouds, will be frozen forever. Memories slip away with time, I'd tell him. But photographs, they're permanent.

But I don't say any of that when I look back at him. Instead, I take out the photograph again, of the clouds rolling and tumbling across the sky. Sun like a halo over the hills, trees waltzing with each other to a sudden gust of wind. A few tiny pixels on my phone.

"Why?" my brother asks again.

"Well," I say, not bothering to hide my smile, "why not?"

A Kind of Fairy Tale

Once upon a time, an exceedingly long time ago (and in a parallel dimension too, so don't bother trying to trace these characters) there lived a beautiful princess. She was beautiful. And she was a princess. All her life, people pandered to her because of her beauty. Her parents granted her every desire—ponies, castles, playmates, golden shoes, pretty dresses— never once thinking that their actions could affect her in any negative way. But, as in all good fairy tales, they did. She became a spoiled brat.

Her name was whispered across the land by mouths that hid behind hands, it travelled over the seas on tiny slips of paper surreptitiously folded in bottles. Soon, everyone in the entire world seemed to know what a detestable person she was. Some, they say, packed their bags and moved as far from her kingdom as they could. Others—mainly princes, because princes are weird like this—packed their bags and moved as close as possible.

You see, while the princess was a brat, a bully, a rascal, an imp, a wretch, a whippersnapper, a minx and a monster, she was also rich and beautiful. Hence the influx of princes.

Some were turned away at the gate to her lands, others were let through, while still others climbed trees and ladders to evade the guards and seek the princess in their own way. It was like a cloud of tadpoles swimming towards scrumptious tadpole food.

However—because there always is a juicy *however* in a fairy tale—everyone seemed to have forgotten one person: the one person who would change everything, and bring this spoiled princess's good fortune to an end.

His name was Count Iniquitous. For those who didn't own a thesaurus, Count Iniquitous hung a sign on his gate reading: *Iniquitous* [ih-**nik**-wi-t*uh* s] *adjective: grossly unfair and morally wrong.* Count Iniquitous believed this to be very clever, and often sat in a large room by himself, and laughed about it.

Count Iniquitous fancied himself not a villain (although he is, for the purpose of this fairy tale) but rather a bringer of justice, a thwarter of evils, and a dispenser of retribution. He was wrong, but he had no friends to tell him so.

Count Iniquitous was among those who heard tell of the beautiful princess. A small ladybird, laden with the weight of the paper it was carrying, dropped a scroll on his head one afternoon, made a rude sign at him with its legs, and buzzed away. Being an avid reader, of course Count Iniquitous read the scroll. Then he burned it because he did so hate spoilt brats.

And there was lit the fire of retribution in his soul. He dropped to his knees and, after wincing a little at the sudden shock to his joints, made a vow to himself to rid the Earth of this princess. He vowed to make her so dead that even her own mother wouldn't recognise her. He vowed to use her heart-strings to string his violin—well, he didn't actually think that; I added that in for the story. He only thought the first one, but his objective was clear: kill the princess. (Or put her out of action nicely and humanely, because that's the sort of man he really wanted to be.)

Vow made, soul shivering, Count Iniquitous packed his bags, cast a spell to make himself look like a prince, and set off for the princess's castle.

Not far away, and coincidentally wearing exactly the same jacket, Prince Virtue was doing precisely the same thing, albeit with no urge to kill roiling in his gut. The only thing in there was an apple, and apparently apples don't like to roil.

And so, that day, two men, each with a completely different objective, set off towards the castle—one carrying a dagger and the other a rose.

Meanwhile, the princess, like all good fairytale princesses seeing off the hordes of princes, was staring out the window, waiting for the one man who could truly win her heart of stone.

Count Iniquitous decided he didn't very much like travelling. He'd set out from his doom-ridden castle with veritable bucket-loads of good intentions—well, sort of—only to be thwarted by a sudden downpour of rain. He was cold, wet, miserable, and about fifty miles from his destination. Horses, Count Iniquitous decided, had their uses, after all. Suddenly, he was drawn out of his sad, cold thoughts by a shout.

"Say! You there! Bedraggled person!"

Count Iniquitous turned, incredulous. Galloping towards him, hooves thudding against the sodden ground—not a loud thudding mind you, but a sort of hello-may-I-help-you-aren't-I-nice thudding—was a horse. This horse, white, impressive, very much befitted the armour-clad prince sitting astride its back. (It is impossible for princes to sit *on* horses. They can only ever sit *astride* them.) The prince in question had been the one to call out, and it was he who spoke again now.

"You look a bit down, my friend. May I inquire as to your destination? You look as though you could benefit from a ride."

Count Iniquitous, under normal circumstances, would have cursed this wretched prince off his horse, stolen it, and galloped away. Unfortunately, he didn't know how to ride horses, and this one seemed particularly terrifying. Count Iniquitous did his best to look approachable.

"I most certainly could, young man. I'm headed for the princess's castle."

"Would this be the beautiful Princess Valerie?"

"It would."

"And what is your business with her?"

"Oh, I'm the villain. I'm just dressed like a prince for the purpose of disguise."

"Ah, I see. So you're going to try and kill her with some nefarious device such as poison or a curse, upon which occasion I shall burst through a conveniently placed door and stop you, whereupon she will swoon into my arms and fall madly in love with me?"

"That's correct. Would you mind awfully if I just tagged along?"

"Not at all, good chap! Climb aboard!"

Count Iniquitous thought this very good news indeed. Evil, after all, is necessary, because where would all the heroes be without villains? On the dole, knowing heroes. So he swallowed his pride and climbed up onto the horse's back. The horse—whose name was Gerald, but no one ever found this out because horses can't talk—didn't much like having Count Iniquitous on his back, but he couldn't say so, because, remember, horses can't talk. So he kept quiet, and at a nudge in his side, continued trotting towards the distant shadow of the princess's castle.

Now feeling much more in a deathly mood, Count Iniquitous decided it was time to commence small talk.

"Weather's awful today, isn't it?"

"It most certainly is. And how are you faring?"

"Very well, thank you. How is your mother?"

"She's very well, thank you for asking."

Gerald, who had nodded off when the weather was mentioned, gave a sudden whinny. Well, he actually said, "Look up, you slimy, fly-ridden b**tards!" But as he was a horse, and horses can't talk (remember?) it sounded like a whinny.

Glancing only briefly at the looming tower that, well, *loomed* before them, Prince Virtue patted his steed's neck. "Good girl, Lady. Kneel."

Gerald almost pointed out that his name wasn't Lady, but decided it wasn't worth the bother and knelt down instead.

With a thump, Count Iniquitous slid off the horse's back. "Right-o. I'll just toddle off to the back of this tower, find a mysterious way in, and then I'll linger around a convenient doorway to her room, ready to burst in and cause havoc. I'll see you there, good chap."

"Most certainly will, my friend! And I most certainly cannot wait to see you out of your disguise. I'm sure you're simply fabulous."

Then they went their separate ways, both with a single objective in mind: the princess.

Prince Virtue was most surprised to find a front door. In fairy tales, there's never a front door. There isn't supposed to *be* a front door. How else is the prince going to prove his manliness other than by climbing up a stone wall, clinging to vines, yet still somehow arrive in a pristine state at the princess's room? It was quite ridiculous.

However, Prince Virtue decided that this front door was rather convenient, and also that he would make the most of it. So he opened it and went in.

As this was all very anti-climactic, Prince Virtue donned his helmet and grunted a bit, to add pleasantly heroic sound effects to his ascent of the stairs. Shadows appeared on the walls, and as he closed in, step by step, on the beautiful princess, green smoke curled menacingly around his ankles. (It didn't, but for his sake pretend it did. Makes the story more interesting.)

The closer he got to the princess, the stronger the thudding in his chest became, until it was louder than his footsteps. So absorbed was he in the sound of his heart, he almost didn't notice the princess's door in front of him. Prince Virtue didn't approve of easy entry, but decided there was no point complaining to the Fairytale Etiquette Committee for so small a problem.

From under the princess's door came a sudden dramatic rolling of drums, then a shattering and a scream. (The scream was shattering too, but for the sake of smooth storytelling I'll leave that out.) Prince Virtue steeled himself on one foot and lifted the other dramatically. With a pleasantly impressive *crack*, the door burst open, and the beautiful Princess Valerie fainted into his arms. Laying her gently to one side, Prince Virtue brandished his sword and charged into her room.

"I command you to show yourself!"

Count Iniquitous looked frazzled. "Awfully sorry, I didn't have time to hide. Would you mind awfully just saying that again in a moment?"

"Oh no, not at all."

Prince Virtue averted his eyes as Count Iniquitous wriggled behind the lacy pink curtains.

"Ready?"

"Certainly. Do continue."

With a pleasantly impressive *crack*, the door burst open, and the beautiful Princess Valerie fainted into his arms. Laying her gently to one side, Prince Virtue brandished his sword and charged into her room.

"I command you to show yourself!"

An iniquitous rustling sounded from the pink lacy curtains in the corner of the room. Prince Virtue felt Princess Valerie clasp his upper arm, her nails digging into his flesh. Together, they stood stalwart in the doorway as red light filled the princess's bedroom and cast shadows that danced like people on the floor. (They were actually doing the boogie, but that has nothing to do with the story. They just wanted you to know.)

Count Iniquitous emerged amidst a clash of drums, face lit up by the lightning that now flashed through the tiny room. He radiated evil and bad cologne. "Get your hands off the princess! She is my property!"

Prince Virtue flung himself in front of the princess. "Never! Thou art a villain and a bitch!"

There was a short silence.

"I meant that thou art a villain and a dog! You shall never have the princess! She is mine to protect!"

"MWA HA HA!!! That is what *you* think! But I, with the power of exclamation marks and capitalisation, shall defeat you and claim the princess as my own!"

Count Iniquitous readied himself for battle, sparks fizzing from his hands. The sound of a sword sliding from its scabbard grated against Prince Virtue's ears but he stood steady, lowering the point to the Count's chest. They were just seconds away from defeating each other when a voice piped up from behind Prince Virtue.

"I don't actually belong to anyone, thank you very much."

Count Iniquitous, Prince Virtue and the narrator of this story stopped doing what they were doing and stared at her. In a parallel dimension, someone with an eraser was scrubbing madly at a page, changing the classic fairytale words and putting new ones into her mouth.

Princess Valerie stepped into the room, fabulously brushing stray lightning from her sleeve. She tore open her dress and stepped out of it, to reveal combat clothing and a sheathed dagger.

"I was never meant to be a princess, but I never had any choice." She eyed the other two. "That's the reason I'm so terrible. I was meant to be a hunter. Cheerio, chaps!"

With that, she flung open her window and leapt into the air outside.

Count Iniquitous clapped and dropped to the ground. Impressive hovering was tiring, and his legs were still hurting from the ride on the Prince's horse. "I am so very glad I didn't have to kill her. I'm not really a murderer. All I ever wanted to do was cultivate plants. Is flower-arranging so bad?"

Prince Virtue let his sword clatter to the floor. "And I always felt happiest designing clothes, hence my fabulous outfit. Say, Snookums, wanna start a flower slash clothing business and pursue our own interests instead of conforming to fairytale standards?"

Count Iniquitous flung himself into the Prince's arms. "Take it away, Sweet Cheeks."

And while they didn't gallop off into the sunset or the sunrise, but rode away from the sun's glare to the nearest teashop, their ending wasn't unhappy. They, of course, lived happily ever after.

And so, by the way, did Gerald.

ROSA FLAHERTY

A Happy Ending

I don't want a fairy ending
like the one in the books
where I lose my shoes
and fall in love just through looks
it's not the story for me

I don't want a sad ending
where I never find my shoes or get out of these blues
or wake up to the birds singing
it's not the story for me

I don't want a normal ending
where I live happily ever after
and my days are filled with laughter
I'd look like the Joker
it's not the story for me

I don't want to save the world
(well maybe I do)
or have my hair curled
for the pretty ball next week

I don't want to be weak
I want to kick down doors
and leave my enemies on the floor
but not really kill anyone
(you get what I mean?)

So maybe the ending for me
is one I find myself
where nothing is absolutely free
and I always have my shoes on

For the Lost

There she is, the one without a smile. If you wait you'll see—ah, there! She's trying again. Her lips curl upwards, her eyes crinkle slightly, but it's wrong. Her eyes don't sparkle or shine with joy; instead, they remain shadowed and empty. Her mouth is a stuttering grimace. She realizes that she can't smile. But she can't stop trying, either. Her life demands a multitude of smiles.

The princess is twenty, still searching for a husband. She doesn't want to have a husband but it's a tradition of the kingdom to be allowed sovereignty only after marriage. Thanks to her late father, she has to float from court to court, waiting. But her lack of a smile turns all the princes away. For all their declarations of love, once they realize they can't make her smile—truly smile, not grimace—they drop off, uncomfortable in a role where she doesn't follow the old patterns. In this world, where godmothers bless beauty on every child in the nobility, her kind of ugliness can't be accepted.

It happens that the princess loses a suitor to yet another kitchen-maid, and she curses her situation. Because she wants her kingdom ever so much she isn't just a hollow smile; she wants to bring it into a new age, to send off explorers and build new roads to trade with the East. But she can't do anything, even though she believes she's twice as clever as the court official who is holding the throne in her stead. So she decides to change the game: she runs away. She can't just run away anywhere: with her travelling from court to court, most people know who she is. Instead, she decides to go across the sea. The escape is uninteresting, since it was so perfectly planned. No one stops her as she walks down the docks to find the new boat she ordered two months ago. She has also employed a boy to help her sail it. She doesn't intend to die tragically on her epic journey just because she doesn't know how to sail, thank you very much.

As she walks down to the boat, she imagines the court official squirming at losing the future queen and failing the kingdom. She believes he could have done more for her—worked towards her aims, rather than above them. That's what she tells herself, anyway. It sounds better than an immature *he wouldn't listen to me*. So this is her small act of revenge. Now life, along with the boy from the boat, calls her. She climbs aboard and they sail off on a light breeze.

Across the sea is the land of magic, where the faeries lived. It isn't—not quite—a real place, and definitely not where humans usually went. The princess's first idea was to ask for a real smile, so she could marry. That lasted about a second before she chastised herself for being so pathetically meagre in her dreams. So she thought some more. Every princess married a prince. She didn't want or need to be like all of them.

So she thought about her real dreams. About trading with the East, expanding the kingdom, reaching beyond the old contracts and superstitions. She decides that she would be the first queen to trade across the sea. There are stories throughout the land of minor trading enterprises, but never anything on a large scale. She would succeed, and then her kingdom would welcome her back to the throne, husband or not.

The further from land they sail the more vicious the wind grows, but since the boy is happy and shouting, she assumes that there's no problem yet. She helps him as much as she can, and they're shouting back and forth against the wind and she's starting to think this could be fun. Later, when the sea is calm and still, she asks him if he knows how long it takes to reach the land across the sea.

He shrugs. "Of course not. No one knows that."

"Will it take longer than a month? We don't have supplies for longer than that."

He shrugs again. "I don't know."

"Why not? Surely people have tried before." She knows they have—it's in the legends.

"Yep, but they've never come back to tell me."

"You are strange. You agree to a voyage across the sea, when you think that it is unlikely you will return. For what?"

The boy looks out to the sea. "I just wanted an adventure," he says quietly.

Thirty-three days later, when they're getting desperate, the boy spots the shore, and calls out, "Land, land!"

They pull up on an empty beach covered with speckled black sand. It's noon already. The princess looks around her.

"Did you hear that?" the boy asks.

"What?"

"Soft music. Laughing. It's like…." The boy runs off. She sighs, and follows him. She can't hear the music but she doesn't want to split up, either.

"It's probably the faeries, you know," he says. "We'll get to see our first faerie!" He finally comes to a halt, saying, "It ended."

"We've still hit gold," she says, pointing to the spring of fresh water gushing out of the rocks in front of them. They drink. It is delicious and cold, with an aftertaste that she can't identify.

"Is this wise?" she asks, pausing. "Drinking the water?"

"Why not?"

"If a faerie song led us here, isn't that like eating faerie food and drink?"

The boy rolls his eyes. "Well, I don't plan to die of thirst," he says.

"Just die of something else, then."

"Come on. It wasn't offered and besides, the rules could be different here."

She shrugs. "Maybe."

For a week, they see no one. They go fishing, and gather berries and roots from the forest. Gradually, they start to go into the forest by themselves, collecting wood, foraging, exploring how far the forest reaches. They haven't found an edge yet, apart from the beach. And that's why the princess is alone when she sees it.

The first faerie she meets smiles at her. It folds its arms—slender and casual—and sits at the base of an oak tree. The princess greets it. It continues to smile, and as she waits for it to reply, she realizes it is the most beautiful smile she has seen, full of wisdom and age and kindness. It seems to demand that she should smile back and she tries, she really does. But it fails, and suddenly the faerie's face drops into an exact replica of the princess's own empty attempt. The copy is so perfect she jumps back in shock. She knows—she's smiled into the mirror for hours, trying to find that missing something that everyone else seems to have. The faerie stands up abruptly, uncrosses its arms, reaches out for her. And she runs. She is terrified. She saw the menace, the glee in the faerie's eyes, knew her own weakness, her terrible hunger for a true smile.

The faerie doesn't follow her, and when she dares to look back, its eyes are closed and it is sitting at the base of the tree again.

Back at the campsite, the boy plies her with questions about the faerie. He has a weird lack of fear in this not-our-land. He picks up on her genderless pronoun and grills her on that. She lets the detour happen because she doesn't want to talk about her fear. She has crossed an entire ocean and someone smiles at her, and she will never feel truly safe again. She shivers and can't blame it on coldness.

"Did someone walk over your grave?" the boy asks.

The second faerie laughs at her. This time the boy is with her, and he's endlessly enchanted. He whispers to her that it is a lady. She isn't so sure. With magic, perhaps faeries don't bother with gender. And the strange thing is that she would assume that he is male if she had to, not female like the boy did. The eye of the beholder, indeed.

This faerie doesn't show the malice of the first. It grabs their hands and pulls them until they reach a circle of dark grass. Now the boy looks uneasy. Excited as he is, everyone knows the primordial lessons taught by no one and everyone. Beware of shadows and dark places. Don't walk off the path. Circles are always magical and sometimes dangerous.

The faerie notices their unease and shakes its head. The princess straightens her spine. If they are trapped now, then they are trapped. She might as well be brave about it this time. But the faerie laughs, shaking its head again. It pulls the boy again—the princess has twisted free—until he is outside the circle. Then it pulls him in again. She doesn't quite trust this, so she tries it by herself. It works, even without the faerie. So they follow it, and soon there are other faeries around them and everyone is dancing, and the air breathes in wind-pipes. The boy is babbling in her ear about the grass circle and how the rules here must be different from other lands, but he is danced away from her and she is alone. The laughter is holding her heart and she wants to smile, but she will not ruin this with her smile.

It is night, and the others start to slip away into the darkness in groups of two and three, linked by whispers. The princess finds the boy again. He is sitting on the grass, staring at his hands. A new faerie is sitting next to him. Again, it looks male to her. He has long red hair shifting to true gold in the moonlight, dark skin and an arm wrapped around the boy's shoulders. She steps back; it doesn't seem right to intrude. But the faerie looks up and beckons her over, with fingers that are curled around the boy's shoulder. She sits down in front of them.

Eventually, the boy lifts his head and looks at her. "I saw everything," he says, with both the wonder of the young and the tired eyes of those who know that seeing everything is only a burden. His gaze grows blank and the faerie rests his head softly on the boy's neck. The princess feels a tinge of jealousy at whatever the boy saw, that she did not see. The boy falls asleep and the faerie adjusts to allow them to lean more comfortably into each other.

"Who *are* you?" the princess asks, though none of the faeries has spoken to her so far. The faerie blinks, then sighs after a couple of seconds of staring at her. He strokes the boy's hair, and it turns grey where he touches it. When she is just about to shout a warning to the boy, the grey flicks back to brown again.

"Age?" she asks, once she realises he's trying to answer her question. He clenches his fist and opens it again. An apple sits there, dusty-rust gold and dark red. She reaches out and takes it. She bites into it, forcing back the warning bells of never-eat-faerie-food. She wants to understand. And then she does.

"Autumn." He nods and loses interest in her, watches the boy sleep. She eats the apple, lets the first chill touch her skin, and wonders how she ever thought to come here and trade. It feels—not quite a child's dream, because she is not a child—but a silly dream all the same, based on the idea that this land would be the same as home, just with a bit more magic. Faerie folk are not human. It took her too long to understand that, not just to know it. The only reason they ever trade is for their own amusement. They are not human, foolish princess.

The princess talks to the boy one day about how the faeries never talk and he bursts out laughing at her. It's so nice to hear his laughter rather than the high laughter of the faerie folk that she forgets to be angry.

"Of course they talk," he finally manages to say. "You don't think they're just animals do you?"

"They talk to you, then."

"Not out loud. In my mind."

It is an interesting answer. She knew they must communicate somehow, but had assumed after her efforts that they only talked to each other, not to humans.

"I'm the seventh son of a seventh son," he adds. "Perhaps that's why I can hear them."

"And I am a princess without a smile," she replies. "Doesn't that qualify me?" Really, she knows the answer. A smile is such a minor thing—unimportant to those with smiles, that is. "You never told me that before," she adds.

"Who else would go on a voyage across the sea?"

This faerie she finds in a little corner of the world. It appears out of nowhere, but since they all do that, she isn't surprised. It waves its hand at her and smiles. She tells herself there are worse things in this world than the lack of a smile, and pushes down her fear to smile back. The faerie giggles—she has never heard a faerie without majesty and it's strange—and claps its hands together.

It is true, she hears. *You really can't smile!*

She stares at the faerie in shock. "You're talking to me."

It nods. *You see, I'm the only one who can give life*, the voice continues. *I would wait until my time but you—you are such a treasure. I know someone who will love you—I'm surprised you haven't met already. Come, come!*

The princess looks backwards, searching for the boy.

He'll be fine, the faerie says. *He's like one of us now.*

So she follows the faerie, feeling leaden and clumsy in comparison to its dancing, graceful steps. She watches carefully the way grass grows under its feet on stone paths, the way the breeze around it smells sweet. Life.

"You're Spring," she says.

Indeed, indeed, the faerie calls back. *But onwards, lass!*

Slowly, the light fades into dull black-and-bruised diffusion. The grass is pale under Spring's feet, cracking with frost. They are going north, she realises, where the cold and the silence lie in the pale light of snow. They are going to see Winter. She wonders what all the other faeries are—there can only be four seasons, after all. Are they lesser beings or simply not in power at the moment? Are they the small things—snow and flowers and ripe fruit?

No, Spring replies. *We are all warriors.* The princess doesn't understand. Spring laughs. *Well, that's what the others tell me. I wouldn't know.*

The princess notices the faerie is walking slowly now, more stiffly. *He never liked me,* Spring laughs. And they are there, at a sparse stretch of ice reaching as far as the eye can see, empty of everything else. She blinks. Is this supposed to be a kingdom?

No, Spring replies. *Winter is alone.*

A hawk flies towards them over the vastness. As it lands, it shifts into a faerie with white hair and pale skin untouched by the warmth of red blood.

What is this? Winter asks, and a strange lethargy smothers her bones. His voice isn't cold as she expected, but far too soft.

I brought a present! Spring says.

I do not need presents.

But she is wonderful—watch! Spring cries, *Smile, sweetheart!* and the princess does, too lethargic to be ashamed once again.

Winter laughs. It isn't high like the others, but deep. *An oddity,* he says. *Thank you.* Then he flicks his hand and Spring collapses silently onto the ice. The princess doesn't move, caught in the fright of prey and the cold wind. Her blood remains slow in her veins.

Come little princess, he says, touching her shoulder. She is sure she is going to die, but instead feels the bones of her body shift and her skin itch.

Two hawks fly off across the ice.

Once upon a wind, she sees the boy again. He immediately recognizes her (oh, the power of seven) and calls out. But it is a mind call and her vision blurs as she lands.

I heard what happened, he cries. *You must be glad—so lucky! I suppose the smile paid off in the end!*

She hasn't thought of her smile for days (weeks, years) because there is no need to smile here. The silence and the cold swallows it whole. But here is the boy, smiling and talking. She wishes he would talk like a human. She tries to reply aloud, but her voice croaks with disuse and she gives up.

What are you doing now? she asks, as if they are still in that place that she cannot quite recall but mourns all the same—distantly, because nothing is immediate in winter; and yet he is still here, so alive, and how does he move so much?

Oh, everything! he replies, with a laugh that hurts her ears. *There is so much to learn here: I never knew there was so much! Right now, I'm researching the history. There's so much of it, it makes the humans seem so primitive with their baby kingdoms. And then I'm going to write it all down and give it to Autumn, then I'm going to talk with Summer to get some magic and—*

What are you doing here?

He looks disconcerted for a moment, but then launches back into it. *Well, the history of Winter, of course, and actually—this is a bit of a secret—I want to talk to Jack Frost. It would be so interesting, and he's like us, so —*

Jack Frost is not like us, she says sharply. *He is too ancient.*

What's age! All that means is that he knows more.

No. It means he has forgotten he was ever human.

Hmm. Well, I shall meet him and decide then!

Perhaps not. He is across the sea at the moment.

That's a pity. I'll talk to Winter anyway and I can wait until he returns. Then we can spend some time together, as well!

He must have come from Spring, she thinks. Nothing else is so excitable. She wonders how long it will be until he falls silent, like all of them.

Follow me, she says, and turning into a bird again, she flies across the ice. She cannot deny him this, even if she wishes to. She has long since realised the world does not care about her wishes. Besides, she doesn't want to be alone. The boy runs alongside her, too fast to be simply human any more.

It starts to affect him as they get closer to Winter. She descends and assumes her human form again because he can't keep up with her. She can hear the familiar whispers falling from the harsh winds; sleep, oh sleep, lie down, so easy, sleep forever.... She pulls him up when he sits down. *Now, you wanted to see Winter, didn't you? You have to finish the journey now.*

Eventually they reach him, with the princess almost dragging the boy along. She is surprised—only slightly, with her dying emotions—to see he is not alone. His sister stands beside him, surrounded by a huddle of humans. So she knows what is going to happen. The sister beckons one of the humans over: *You must be so cold, I know a place with a warm fire for you to stay in.* As soon as the human touches her hand, he crumples to the ground, lifeless. Yet none of the other humans notices this and each member of the huddle is slowly pulled out and killed. The boy quickly looks aside, eyes on the horizon, when he notices the scene. The princess doesn't. It occurs to her that this is simply boring; a spectacle. It doesn't mean anything. The sister turns to the princess and the boy.

Oh, you brought me a treat, sweetie?

He's protected.

Really, the sister says and reaches out her arm—and frowns. *Oh, a seventh son of a seventh son. No fun at all.*

Winter stares at him and does the quick motion with his hand and the boy collapses onto the ice. The princess feels slow rage build in her stomach but Winter shakes his head. *Be calm. I only killed the Spring in him.*

And there, he stirs. She helps him up and sees his eyes are slightly emptier than before, although he still bows and asks a few tentative questions. She thinks she despises him—Winter or the boy, she does not know—and at the thought, Winter glances at her and smiles and she smiles back, empty as each other.

You chose this, Winter says to her. *And this is how it has to end,* and she finds herself saying the words alongside him.

Highlighter Art

Draw me
with wavering lines
in a shade of shy blue
to match the infinite sky.

Add a coat of red
for my heart and my lungs
and maybe yours too.

Use bright green
for my emerald eyes
and outline them with a
smoky purple.

Gently mould me
with a sunflower yellow
and inject me
with liquid so that my skin
is a shade of toughness.

And when you're done
leave my bellybutton and three-quarters of legs
then highlight the rest with
neon pink to let me stand out
from all the other
shades of grey

The Antarctic Flower

Klaus breathed heavily on the icy sheet of glass and wrote NIGHTMARE. It must have been something to do with working in documentaries that made him want to put tabs on everything that happened. This was most definitely a nightmare.

How long had they waited? A year, basically. The whole thing was such a longsuffering process. *Longsuffering*—that was another good word. Klaus scrawled it beneath his fast-fading NIGHTMARE. Yes, this was most definitely *longsuffering*.

The door shrieked as the panels slid open. Another patient stepped out of the Christchurch rain and over the threshold. Klaus didn't even bother to turn his head. He'd been waiting in reception an hour already, with no idea when the medical and dental exams would end.

Antarctica New Zealand had accepted the change, but still, Klaus wondered if anyone knew what a massive spanner this threw in the works of all their plans. Probably not. The enormousness of it overwhelmed even him. He was contemplating the change—the hours of rescheduling plans, of resubmitting profiles, of reorganising the entire transportation of two people to *terra australis nondum cognita* and lots of other words beginning with *re* when he heard the elevator rattle and ding, and a high-spirited chirp at the counter.

"Hi there!" it said, "I've just done my check-up. I was told someone would meet me here?"

Klaus heard the receptionist's soft-tone reply and imagined her gesture towards his back. He spun round. His eyes were met with an onslaught of colour. Throat to feet, she was dressed in complete greyscale, but her eyes were clean jade, her hair a mane of gold, her skin pink and her mouth the hue of raspberries. Her clothes were winter, her face was summer. She grinned a curve of pearlescent teeth, and sang, "Kia ora!"

"Kia ora," he replied, smiling with a bemused relief as he shook her hand. "Cora?"

"Ha!" she laughed, "Cora, yes. That's the name. And you?"

"I'm the person you'll be assistant to on this trip."

"Oh, the big director, huh? What should I call you. ..." Evidently the question was rhetorical. She glanced him up and down and declared, "Bo".

Klaus gave a spluttering laugh. "What?"

"Bo. I'm calling you Bo. Short for bohemian, you know, with your long hair, and everything."

"All right."

She seemed unfazed, and narrowed her eyes into a tease. "That's gonna get pretty gross once it goes a few weeks without a wash, you know."

Resisting the urge to touch his hair, Klaus looked out into the grim weather. "We've got to go and pick up your climate gear first, then we'll head down to the docks. You got your stuff?"

"Yeah." She motioned towards a sparse collection of luggage. "Why the docks?"

He picked up two of the surprisingly heavy bags and nodded towards the door. "To catch our ride."

"You mean we aren't taking the Hercules?"

So she'd done her research. He stormed out across the car park. "We're not flying in that monster. That first kid we picked, who pulled out of the scholarship, really made a mess of everything. This is the busiest time of year. We've had so much bad weather, and with the planes boomeranging back almost every time…" he wiped the hair out of his eyes, unlocked the car and tossed the bags in the back "… there's no room for the two camera crew who got left behind last summer. We're lucky to get a passage aboard the cargo." They fell into the dry warmth of the vehicle, watching the rain slither down the bonnet.

"But that'll take weeks!" said Cora. "I wondered what they meant when they told me the expedition would take longer than 'previously estimated'."

"Well now you know." Klaus rammed in his seatbelt buckle and cranked the engine on. "We'll arrive just in time for them to start conservation on Borchgrevink's hut, so long as the ice doesn't hold us back."

Cora ruffled her chin-length hair all the way to its bushy ends. "Lovely. I've always wanted to meet a penguin colony. And we'll be there to document it all, eh, Bo?"

Klaus gave an involuntary laugh. "Never mind the setbacks, I suppose."

Green Wave's hull hurled itself against the floes and roughly shoved them aside, but when Cora tilted her head over the rail and hung forward, it looked as if the angular chunks of ice were rising to challenge the battered ship.

Flipping back upright, she gazed out upon the endless mosaic of whites and greys, whites and greys and blues. She'd taken hundreds of photos already—capturing the spectacle from this angle and that—running from one end of the ship to the other with a tripod on her shoulder and a vision in her head. She had to compensate for Bo, of course.

"How is he?" she asked one of the passing crew, a man whose broad Australian accent gave her endless entertainment.

He continued to stroll by, glancing at the ocean and the clouds, and commented, "Quiet." It sounded like KWAI-et. Cora didn't know if he meant the head of photography or the seascape.

"Does he need any help?"

The man shrugged. "Warsn't maykin eny sauond."

"I'd better go down and check–"

She was interrupted by a sailor raising one calm finger. "Look."

Cora cried out.

"Poorpisses," the Australian declared.

And they were—wolves of the sea slicing between shards of ice, their enormous black knives rising out of the water in sharp silhouettes of black on white. They were so close Cora could see their sinister, intelligent eyes. Their vast nine-metre bodies slipped above and beneath the surface, a smooth, endless, rollicking wavelength.

"It's an entire pod!" she exclaimed. "Tell them to wait!"

Throwing herself down into the ship's bowels, she tore along the passage to Bo's cabin. The crewman had been right; it was unusually quiet. No moans, no nothing. The door was ajar, and she crept in, ignoring an acrid smell that hung thick enough to slice up and wrap in paper.

Bo was fast asleep, a miserable lump of clothing tossed into a corner of the bunk. Deciding not to disturb his peace, Cora carefully removed the equipment she needed from his seemingly endless luggage. She tiptoed out of the room, slithered along the passage, and dashed up the steps to get onto the deck where she could film the pod of orcas. She intended to do it so well that Bo wouldn't miss a second of it.

Klaus, lurching out of a thick blanket of sleep, stared when he saw the girl crouched on the floor of his cabin.

"What are you doing?"

"I'm sorry," she whispered, even though he was already up. "I didn't mean to wake you."

An awful taste still filled his mouth, and his stomach writhed as though it was alive. Before he could form another thought, liquid flamed up his oesophagus and he was retching, belly folding inside out. Cora was quick to intercept the vomit with a large bucket between her knees, pulling the hair out of Klaus' line of fire. She piled it on top of his head and held it there while he finished emptying the remains of his last meal.

The Australian chose that moment to pop his head around the door and proclaim, "Fuud's up."

He was answered by a heave from Klaus that sent the bucket rattling.

"We'll pass," said Cora.

A grin split the crewman's face. The sight of a chronically seasick thirty-something-year-old, dripping with bile and grizzled with a week-old beard, was something of a joke among the crew—especially when they'd had the calmest weather possible since Lyttelton. It was a blessing for him, the sailor surmised, that the kid student was willing to play nurse. He went away chuckling and shaking his head.

"Thanks." Klaus spat into the bucket and leaned back, exhausted.

Cora handed him a rag to wipe his face with. "Not far to Scott Base now," she assured him. "Though we haven't hit the pack-ice yet. Do you need me to shave your face like I did last time?"

"No." His eyes were closed, his face pale under his dark beard.

"Did you know that you'd get seasick?"

Klaus nodded, without self-pity.

"You must really want to go to Antarctica," Cora smiled, and got up to open the door. "Almost as much as I do."

"Why were you sitting on the floor?"

"Oh, I was meaning to tell you." She whirled, and jumped back onto her stool. "I was just putting away some of your equipment. I've been up on deck filming for hours, Bo; you'll never guess what I saw! I was going to wake you up but then I thought you needed the sleep, and then I wanted to rush back –" Cora stopped suddenly, teetering into the next sentence. "Do you want me to leave you alone?"

"No." Klaus opened his eyes. "Stay. And tell me what happened."

He felt himself growing more and more sick the longer they stayed on the ocean, the closer they were to Antarctica. Cora was swelling with life and energy. For a long time she perched beside him in the cabin, vividly describing the beauty of the ice floes and the stunning majesty of the sea wolves that roamed them, until he felt himself falling into an exhausted, relief-filled sleep.

The next day Bo felt settled enough for Cora to take him on deck. They brought the camera gear in the hope that he might feel strong enough to capture some of his own footage of the frozen world.

Cora noted that it was a stunningly bright day. Bo squinted the moment he stepped into the sunlight, pale as a worm that had lived underground too long. They decided to move astern to catch the seascape as it slid out of reach.

"Isn't it beautiful?" She ran to the rail, gasping out at the steely, monochromatic scenery while Bo set up the camera and tripod. "This is like a dream. It's going to be the highlight of my life. Sometimes I still can't believe I'm actually going, you know?"

Bo gave one of his wry smiles and adjusted the zoom of the lens. The wind bit him across the face. "How do you know you'll like it? Antarctica's not for the faint-hearted. There's nothing there. It's an enormous wasteland of freezing emptiness."

"Don't pretend indifference with me, mister," she leapt up and perched precariously on the edge. "It's an enormous *wonderland* of freezing emptiness. It's like nothing else on the planet. Aren't you excited?"

Bo didn't answer. A photographer at heart, he picked out colour and composition everywhere he went. And here was a perfect image: Cora seemed like an icon in the seascape, with the flat, broad blue of the sky bouncing off the rainbow hues in her face. Everything else was greyscale—blindingly white ice, chillingly dark coats—but Cora was a spot of nodding colour in a bleak world.

"Sometimes I imagine being surrounded by that massive, unbroken, continent-wide silence; the sound of absolutely nothing, a sort of roaring quiet—and it feels so *old*, unchanged. I think she's around us like an ancient great-grandmother, and we've come back to dig up her secrets in this weird world that's dead but never dies. Like she's been alive forever, transcending time."

Bo grinned from behind the eyepiece of his camera. "That's very poetic. People tend to be poetic about Antarctica if they've never lived there."

"*You* haven't!".

"No." He pulled his face away and fiddled with the height of the tripod. "But what do people think of when they imagine people in Antarctica? Bravery, the Heroic Age. Shackleton's trans-Antarctic *Endurance* mission, where they all lived happily ever after. But all the men laying supplies for him on the other side of the continent didn't come out so well. No one cares about them."

"You mean the men on the *Aurora* who sailed in to lay a trail of depots for Shackleton?"

"Exactly. How many died? One on the way back from laying supplies. Their ship blew out to sea in a storm and took all their stuff with it. Two fell through the young ice trying to cross open water to get back to the hut at Cape Evans."

"What's your point? You're annoyed that people don't remember the shocking conditions? All the starvation, scurvy, and storms?"

"I'm saying it's not all fun and games," Bo muttered, squinting through the viewfinder. "We can be poetic as we like about endless worlds that transcend time, right up until everything goes to pot and frostbite sets in."

"You're such a downer, Bo," Cora laughed, but she didn't press. She figured the man must be feeling in horrendously bad shape after weeks of seasickness. Watching him now, the icy air seemed to have revived him, but his eyes were still hollow and sunken. He probably felt closer to those starving men of the *Aurora*'s Ross Sea party: sickly, tired, and weak.

"Tell me more about those men in the expedition, Bo," she insisted, "the ones who didn't make it."

"Says the one moaning about downers."

"*C'mon!*"

So, between the adjustments of his camera and the shifts across deck, Bo talked. He told her about the longest sleigh journey in the world, where Spencer-Smith died of exhaustion and scurvy. He told her about the men stranded at Hut Point, unable to cross the water to rejoin the team at Cape Evans.

He told her about Captain Mackintosh and Hayward, who ignored the protests of the other men and walked desperately out across the ice and into a roaring blizzard. He told her how the men found nothing but tracks leading up to broken floes; and the whole time she wavered before him, nodding her head energetically at the demise of life in a harsh and inhospitable world.

"This place stinks."

Klaus couldn't help but laugh at Cora's first observation upon touching down at Cape Adare. "That's what you get for building a hut in the middle of a massive penguin colony, I suppose."

"Good old Carsten Borchgrevink," Cora giggled, and hopped through the squawking throng of birds. "I wonder if he thought they were cute. I love penguins, but they still stink."

They drew closer to the old, dilapidated hut, which was already surrounded by busy members of the Antarctic Heritage Trust who were setting up shelters. The group planned to camp there for the next few weeks, to begin the incredibly long and technical process of returning the historic site to its former glory.

"He didn't really pick the ideal area, did he," Klaus observed, gazing around at the flatness to the north and the towering, cliff-like peaks looming south of the hut. "Windy and exposed. Can't have been much fun wintering over here."

Cora was already far ahead, bouncing up the slope to where the conservationists were setting up an elaborate Polarhaven. "Hurry up, Bo. Let's set up a time-lapse of them pitching all the tents. It'll look awesome with that background!" She spread her arms, and planted her feet among the stones. Beyond Adare, the six-month-sun was blazing in a sky that was scratched with ice and indifferent to its distant warmth. Klaus turned once again to face the flat, ice-strewn north swarming with penguins and glowing with light.

Somewhere up there a million years ago, he thought, they'd left New Zealand far behind.

"Cora!" Klaus bellowed. "*Cora!*"

The girl's head, grubby after weeks with no wash, appeared above a stack of musty crates encrusted with penguin guano. "What?"

"What are you doing?"

"Checking the lighting. I'm trying to see if −"

After a few muttered words exchanged with the team leader from the Antarctic Heritage Trust, Klaus turned. "We need to pack up. We need to get out of here, now."

"What for?"

"There's a freak storm coming. Scott Base has sent helicopters and ordered us back out of the field before it hits."

"A freak storm?" her incredulous voice echoed from behind the crates. "Well, that's convenient. We're half way there anyway, the tents are down."

"Hurry, Cora," he urged, striding towards her. "A plane's coming to pick up the team and most of the gear, but with all our equipment we'll be on their helicopters."

At near-frenzy, the entire Heritage Trust conservation team began to condense every inch of their belongings. Severe weather warnings in Antarctica were never to be taken lightly, and so what was left of the project's first stage was abandoned in mid-swing—carefully numbered floorboards stowed hastily under one of the bunks, the artefacts selected for special conservation abandoned in the depths of the old storehouse. Take no chances. Leave no room for error.

Hours later, and in howling wind, the group huddled near the edge of the soccer field flattened a hundred years ago by the hands of long-dead men. Most of the team had already been safely flown back to Scott in the Twin Otter before any visible signs of the storm had set in. Klaus detected the distant chup-chup-chup of approaching helicopters, and a surge of relief swept through him. Within minutes, having swallowed the first team, the earliest buzzed out of the air. Ice swirled about in the razz of rotors, adding another blast to the wind that was already lashing mercilessly at the rags of humanity.

The second 'copter landed just as efficiently, engulfed the team, and in turn was engulfed in the broiling wall of white cloud descending on the cape. Adare, Borchgrevink's hut, the remainder of the team, lay open and bare at the collar. The next helo circled cautiously above, tried to land, and teetered at an angle that brought Klaus' heart to his throat.

"They can't land," the team leader yelled above the now furious wind, watching the machine get battered. "It's too dangerous. They can't land. We'll have to shelter in the hut." He waved to the pilot, using his VHF to communicate. It was only he, Klaus, and Cora remaining.

Shelter in the hut. Masked by the wraps of his extreme-weather gear Klaus followed the other two robotically up the slope. Everything was being quickly enveloped by freezing, screaming whiteness. He crammed into the tiny shed, like being packed tightly into the base of a cardboard box and hunched on one of the bunks. A freezing liquid—pure fear—trickled down his veins and through the insides of his arms. His rapidly increasing breath clouded before him and clouded before him and clouded before him.

Cora appeared at his side, turning her bright face up like a pansy. "Here's a bit of life experience. We'll weather out the weather."

It was easy for her to say. Klaus struggled to keep the low animal whine out of his voice as he asked, "Couldn't they see this coming? Is it so hard to forecast a blizzard?"

"Predicting weather is tricky business," the conservation leader said. "You anticipate a wind angle just a little bit wrong, and the difference in the areas affected can be enormous."

"Not totally unexpected, eh, Bo? We knew what we were in for when we came here," the girl chirped, crawling under Borchgrevink's over-large wooden table in the tiny five-by-four room.

When they came here? He'd known more than blizzards. For the first time, Klaus admitted to himself that he'd never wanted to come at all. He hadn't asked to. He'd been employed to come. From the moment he'd opened the letter of approval it had felt like conscription, more than anything else. They'd asked him because he was supposed to know. He *knew* all right—the books, the knowledge, all the history; but it was no more than vicarious. He had never wanted to come to Antarctica. He had never asked to come.

Cora could see it the moment he shuffled onto the floor, legs spread before him, and stared, with hollow, unseeing eyes, at the cloth hanging from an upper bunk. The storm shrieked and clung to the hut, tearing at it wildly with furious, formless fingers. Inside, the temperature was exactly like sitting in an ice cube, dark and cold, wrapped in the madness of a forgotten continent. And Bo sat unmoving in the gloomy darkness, his pale face wrapped in dank, dark hair, responding neither to the storm nor to any evidence of the world around him.

Why was he afraid? They had food. They had fuel. They would last if they didn't screw things up. There was nothing to fear except unlikely death, and death itself was obviously inevitable in the grand scheme of things. She was on the verge of reaching out to lay a hand on his shoulder when there was an enormous thump on the left wall. The door blasted open and slammed shut with reverberating force. A crumpled sound rattled against the gaps in the floorboards.

"What was that?"

"Let me light the lamp." Risking fuel, the conservation leader illuminated the lantern and held it up.

Cora cried out. The leader swore. A figure, blue-skinned and wrapped in a mass of canvas, cotton and sealskin, lurched unsteadily against the floor. His face was overgrown by a beard of clumped hair on cheeks burned to a tough leather. The two hungry, terrified eyes of someone or something somewhere between human and animal, glared around at all of them. He/it quaked with exhaustion, with the cold, and with death.

It was at that exact moment when time literally froze in Cora's mind. The scene crystallised: three figures from the future wrapped in bright cloaks of warm material, their breath distilled in puffs of cloud, one holding the glowing light aloft; the fourth a caveman of emaciated proportions, crinkled like a ball of parchment on ancient floorboards, surrounded by the rusted, dusty memoirs of a hundred years. And the whole swallowed in the mouth of unchanging elements.

Klaus rose on slow feet, swearing softly. "I know him."

"You know him? What do you mean, you know him?" the leader snapped.

"I know him. I know that face." He knew it exactly, from all the printed books he'd studied, in all the websites he'd roamed. His heart slammed within him, hammering against his ribcage. "I know him. I swear, it must be Mackintosh!"

The caveman responded with a strangled cry, eyes filling with confusion and fear. He staggered to his feet, too weak and frozen to utter a word. That starving gaze stumbled with stifled horror across these foreign faces; he twisted, and before they could move, threw himself back into the blizzard.

They all shouted at once and rushed towards the open door. Cora launched herself forward in an ill-timed leap, just as gale-force winds hurled it back and smashed her into the bunk. Klaus cried out and threw himself down beside her.

"What a nightmare," said the leader, heaving the door closed and kneeling to check her pulse. "What a nightmare. But she'll come round. Better get her into a sleeping bag."

"Who's going after Mackintosh?" Klaus asked, dazed.

"It won't be Mackintosh. If I can nab him now, there'll be a chance of his surviving the exposure. He'll be following the lean-to through to the storage hut to see what's there."

Klaus rose to his feet. "I'll get him."

"No, you won't!" the man said forcefully, grabbing onto Klaus's wrist and rising. "I will. I'm responsible for our lives. You take care of her, and don't leave the hut!"

Klaus left the hut.

He regretted it before he left, and he regretted it after. Regret couldn't kill his sense of duty, and he regretted that, too.

Cora was safe; that much he could be satisfied with. He tried to keep his mind on this as he inched his way along the outer wall of what he hoped was the lean-to. The wind screamed in his face and, like a boxer coming from all angles, pummelled him relentlessly with icy snow. He couldn't see. He could feel his throat vibrating, but he couldn't hear his own muffled cries. He didn't even feel like a person any more, not one with a body that could see and speak and hear and feel—because all that existed was a jabbing, pounding, roundabout slamming of angry, voiceless frozen ice lunging at him out of suffocating greyness.

The shed. All he had to do was get to the storage shed and find the leader—that blasted leader who went and got himself swallowed in the mouth of a raging wasteland leaving *him* to play the hero! And if he wasn't there, well, what was there to do?

On that note, the storm struck him across the face, wrenching away all the security and hope and everything the touch of the wall beneath his glove meant, sending him reeling into formlessness. The ground leapt up to pound him. Klaus ground his teeth in terror, and twisted round to grope for his lifeline. It wasn't there.

At first, he felt faint. Then the ferocity of the storm overtook him. What were they doing, chasing a ghost of the past through the madness of a lost continent? Would that save him now? Now, and tomorrow? Klaus squeezed his eyes shut and stared at the gloating twins of death and his own irritating mortality. It was only much later, looking back from a point six metres back and two high, that he could see the bloom—and not only her, but himself.

Our Land

This is a story which may or may not be true. Judge it as you will. It's about a girl called Abby who lived in the town of Orakaunui, where everyone knew everyone else, the bush was swallowing the bungalows, and no one cared about the time because it passed in such meagre droplets. Abby had lived all her life in Orakaunui and spent her days exploring the bush. If the incident had not happened, doubtless she would have exhausted the bush by the time she was fifteen and followed the restless footsteps of her contemporaries to Auckland. But it happened, and so Abby never left.

But we need more setting, don't we? Family: mother nursing a cold beer on the porch, father long gone, older sister gone to Aussie, little brother rolling with the dog in the sun and the rain. School: ignored by Abby apart from the occasional attempt to attend before the dry boredom of the classroom gave her the conviction never to return. The teacher complained about this, but mother complained right back—*Let the child be*. Teacher left bitter, saying *I tried my best, but some people....* Abby's favourite person: Grandpa, who swore blue he was one year under 200. In Abby's eyes, he knew everything. He taught her all the trees and what plants to eat, and once went fishing with her. He warned her about the boars that tore through the bush and said never to get behind a mother and child. Abby tried this one day with mother and little brother but mother only took another sip of her beer and told Abby to buy pizza for tea and there was money in the box in the kitchen.

Grandpa told Abby about the moa, the gigantic flightless birds who ruled the bush in the days before the dogs and boar and everything else came to New Zealand. He beckoned her closer and whispered in her ear, *I saw one once*.

After that, Abby's life goal was to find a moa. When she went to school to tell this to the class, the teacher told her not to be ridiculous, *moa were extinct*. Abby said *no one has tried hard enough*. The bush was so big that anything could be lost and never found again.

Her search started in the summer, when the pohutukawa trees displayed fine red threads and a rosella parakeet came visiting from Auckland Zoo. Since the bush was cooler than the burnt yellow lawns, she slipped away into it every day. She searched every inch, mapping the terrain out in her head, naming places to remember them. Here were the weka-nest and where-Tony's-pig-liked-hiding, and the dog-run-at-night. But eventually she knew everything in a day's walk and she still hadn't found a moa. So she took some money from the box in the kitchen and told mother she would be camping for a few days; and mother made sure she had enough warm clothes, waved goodbye and went and sat on the porch again.

This is where Abby's story really begins.

On the first day she walked due north into the bush, reaching the outskirts of her known territory at when-the-moon-rises. She set up her tent, unrolled her sleeping bag and set up a stove made from an old can. She ate, then went to sleep. She dreamed of moa crashing past her, all of them in a great hurry to escape or to reach something. She didn't manage to touch any of them.

The second day was long, but Abby occupied herself by talking to a tui that was following her. It left her at the end of the day, and Abby wished it good luck.

On the third day, she found a clue: moa footprints. An adult, of course, wouldn't have believed their eyes but Abby, luckily, was only a child, so she followed the footprints. She was almost too excited to sleep that night—she didn't want to lose the moa. But she was tired, and it was too dark to go further safely. So she slept.

On the fourth day, she found the moa. The tracks had become more recent, so she had climbed a nearby tree. And then it appeared, walking between the trees. Its eyes were small and hard, like shining stones. It flicked its head when a twig cracked under Abby's hand, and looked straight up at her. Abby was sure it was the most beautiful thing she had ever seen. She climbed down the tree—the moa's imperious glare seemed to demand that—and walked up to it, hand extended. Neither was afraid. She stroked its neck, the feathers small enough to be fur. Then Abby heard voices and she wanted to cry with anger at the intrusion but the moa did not run. Two pale children emerged from the bush.

Who are you?

We are here.

I found a moa.

There are many.

But they're extinct.

You are from the after-time, the children say, *where many things are dead. But this is the before-time. The time before our land changed, the time where it never changes.*

And they ran off together to find more moa.

Who were the children? Let me tell you. Before the Europeans the land belonged to the Maori. Before the Maori there were the Mori Ori, some early stream of Pacific voyagers before the Maori left Hawaiki. And before the Mori Ori there were the children of the forest, pale things, always with the reddest hair. The Maori saw them, spoke of them in their stories. Their reflections blur too easily in the bush today but they are still there, covered in layers of centuries, sea-glass murky.

That is why the mother did not despair as the search for Abby deepened into many nights. Grandpa told her the children of the forest would favour Abby, with her red hair. Then, one day, she saw Abby. Saw her but could not touch her, could not pull her out of the time in which the bush children lived. So for a while she watched Abby play with her new friends, and never told anyone but Grandpa. Then she went home and warned little brother never to go into the bush without her.

Every year, they both go into the bush, hands held tight, and watch Abby. But as the years pass, Abby becomes paler and harder to see. Then one year she turns from them completely and walks away, her moa beside her. Little brother and mother never see her again. They never forgot her either—their moa girl.

When he's older, little brother wonders if mother made it all up so he wouldn't be sad. He still prefers the moa story.

Stolen Fruits

In my corner of the woods
the tooth fairy brought a single dollar
hidden in a matchbox
because money was a death match
that always went out before the candles were lit

Coming of age meant learning to drift
from doorway to porch to street corner
like some tipsy patupaiarehe
a barefoot beauty
with rouged cheeks pressed against the dashboard
and a cup that was never empty
or full

Fragilely blossoming into a misshapen angel
blessed enough to be sharing a stale pastry
with the man who screams at cars
they've got him on meds you know
I saw him shaking his fists at a low hanging cloud
he said it was his mother in her nightgown and pearls

Half baked cakes comprising drunken fruits and other sins
family recipes with too much of this and too little of that
eaten with stained fingers behind other people's berry bushes
the bugs on your skin like bullet holes
from the moon man's gun

If I was the forest's own drunken nymph
then you must have been a ponaturi
a salt-stained mirror twin from beyond the blue
gnarled and damp with claws to drag me down
and a mouth filled to bursting
with second hand sugar
and first-hand remorse

When you told me about how the white man came
I pictured one giant entity
a misty tyrant as big as the sky
crushing our ancestors with white noise
and mouths stiffened to speechless
with the overbearing dryness of cotton wool

Winter is just one long game of blind man's bluff

you had said after the moon men left us reeling
A season of groping at wool and flesh
at tongue and teeth under snow and sleet
A season of cracked lips behind cracked glass
wai wherowhero running down our chins
each stream cowering
from the taunting antithesis of the sun

Patupaiarehe: Maori for fairy, traditionally believed to have fair skin and pale hair. Said to live in the bush.
Ponaturi: Maori for sea goblin, similar to Patupaiarehe. Thought to have large claw-like talons.
Wai wherowhero: red water, can be linked to blood in waterways after a battle.

NATASHA GEORGE

Ignorance is Bliss

Ivy inches across the steel gate
its hands gripping the bars,
its leaves peering through.

With a gentle graze of my fingertips,
I touch this dark beauty.

It inches back further into the dark,
revealing the padlock.
Sliding in the rustic key,
I hear that comforting *click*.

Closing the creaking gate behind me,
I walk into this wild land of enchantment

where acres of trees make the mountains dense,
and meadows of flowers perfume the air.
Fireflies become the stars,
to comfort the lonely moon.

It's dark here,
but beautiful too.

Nothing's scarred by war,
but then again, this place has never experienced change.
It's all an illusion I keep replaying in my mind,
and maybe,
just maybe
I don't want to wake this time.

ROSE MCCULLOCH

Maui's Beacon

They told me I could be anything, so I donned my boots and pack and jingled the chain on the dog's leash and, slamming the door resolutely behind me, went to be Maui.

My prey seemed laughably close, as if an effortless reach to pluck a fierce white eye from an aloof dome and bury it in the ground to light a path would lead me to a great, dead animal. Like Maui, I cast my net and felt it pulled easily from my failing hands, like a spider web of life. I climbed to the highest mountain on the highest part of the planet and opened my mouth to swallow him whole, but he drifted indifferently to the edge of the world and disappeared. He did not look back as I fell to the ground, wracked with hollow loss.

I lay on the ground as the gold sovereign rose again, turning the hills in front to smooth curves of pure black spotted with dwarfed lights like a small sky. The sky was orange, vanishing to blue in a blend no paint on this earth could re-create. At the right angle, with my eyes half closed, my eyelashes became polar bear hair, each lash catching the light and flashing a muted silver rainbow into my eyes, a window into Eden's tributary.

Maui did not win this colourless ball. He left it. He failed. He returned with a *kete* and all the mana it could hold, and inside he kept a circlet of *harakeke* studded with silvery fish scales and shards of paua shell, and other things that shone and glistened. And no one told him that his prisoner had an escaped soul that lit his way home.

I could be anything, couldn't I, so I waited for my laughing victor to blaze his path and leave the world to the dark and twisted creatures inside us. And when he did, I went to her, the pockmarked disc of silver that had the dog on the leash throwing back his head and offering up, with every tooth ivory and a rolling pink tongue, a wrenching agony of noise to that all-powerful reflection of my victor. Of course, how could I not have known that her quiet beauty and dignity, her constant inconsistency, was even more beautiful than her beacon? The bleached Sun lives only to light the path of our nameless moon. She is the prize!

Humour me, dub Maui a fool. The light is only there to point the eye to look to the other end for the item to sling with woven nets and cast down. I went, dog capering at my heels, to meet his commander. The nets, lost in the heat of the sun, wrapped easily around the cool moon and down she came, crashing through the heavens once freed from her orbit. A dusty, cratered rock lies in my field, her silver stripped, her smoke and mirror waxing and waning vanished.

Her dull-eyed, graceless bulk demands the eye. This is not she. In the sky, the shy, beautiful creature that basks quietly in the glow of her devoted beacon is gone. A void of space remains. This is not she. The dog dances, barks. She can no longer draw a howl from him. The sun searches for a target. This is not she. And my heart… my heart is a small, dead animal. If I could bury it in the ground, as *utu*, I would.

AMY DAWBER

Ancients

Its eyelids flicker. Once, twice, its gaze set in full force on our family. We stand silent. Not in defeat, but with an ancient pride behind us. With a grumble and a roar, it comes to life and moves towards us.

Once, we were small. We would have been no bigger than a nail on your finger. To us, it was a millennium ago, but we remember it well. Not enough has changed in the years since then for us to forget our beginning. That is, until now.

In the damp and the dark our journey began. Together yet alone, we were unsure and frightened of the impervious darkness. It not only surrounded us, it suffocated our bodies and penetrated our thoughts. The darkness always shifted with the movement of others. We could not see these earth-shakers, as we are blind to the world; however, our other senses are strong. Especially our sense of fear. Each tremble of the darkness carried through us and with it we shook like the leaves that would eventually drop off us in the autumn.

Day after day, we trembled with fear of the unknown until, finally, the trembles built up to a single tremor that seemed to shake the whole world. And then, something felt different, felt new. More than ever before, we were connected to the earth and the creatures living there with us: we had grown roots. That was when we knew we were more—more than the darkness and this small existence.

After that, we were no longer scared. We grew with the earth-shakers, the land-walkers and the leaf-friends around us. We grew and grew and grew, and then we were born. Escaping the darkness, we reached to touch the sky. At first the light was blinding, but we had never felt more alive. One by one we appeared, shy and bashful in the new world. Our senses were overwhelmed with everything we could feel—the inconsistent variation of the warmth and the cold, the wet drops that we so desired which came from above and the feeling of something rushing by without there being anything to cause movement. We could feel the soft brushes of the land-walkers' fur against our fragile bodies, and the earth-shakers' small but powerful limbs exploring our new presence in their oversized world.

Those were the glory days, when life was exciting and new. We felt the world expand with us and we grew more roots, more connections, each day. We felt that we knew it all. We were just saplings to the world, but to ourselves, we were already the giants of the forest.

We could feel the ripples of change begin when they arrived. They were a part of nature just as we all were, yet disconnected. They had forgotten the basis of their kind and had lost their own roots. We felt the earth move as they built their shelters. We felt the pain of our cousins as the intruders removed what they wished for the good of themselves. We felt our leaf-friends' cries as their branches were stripped bare of the food that had taken weeks to grow.

However they weren't all bad. There were gentler touches from the withered hands of those who remembered a time when their race brought more than destruction and greed; and there were playful grasps from the soft hands of those who remained untouched by

44

selfishness and only felt the warmth in their hearts. We felt the joy they left in the world when they would climb the branches of our elders and jump amid our leaves.

Many generations have passed since the first, and the numbers continue to grow. We have become numb to the quivers resulting from ruin. We stand, silent and proud but forgotten, as we have for centuries. Until now.

In all our time here, we have never felt more united. We have stood tall and strong, waiting for the moment to arrive. The journey was too quick: it came too suddenly, just as all undesired things do. It seemed as if the whole forest, land-walkers and earth-shakers included, took a collective breath as it came closer and closer. And then, it halted. Why had it stopped now? To tease us, to draw out our agony? But then, there was a slight brush, the lightest of touches, on every one of our trunks. Linked hand by hand, they, our neighbours who had so forgotten us, were protecting our very beings, standing silent, tall and strong as we were. We were one.

FREDDIE GORMACK-SMITH

The Shipwrecked Sailor's Guide to Settlement

Seawards, there are grey hills, oh Castaway,
made from the million grains of passing seconds and topped
with outlandish flowers.
Take your pick from the graveyard of bleached tree bones.
Make your way to the top of the hills,
using the path overgrown with fiercely jagged brambles.
Once you have found a shady, secluded alcove,
you must take the bones and have them lean, supporting one another.
Though they may slouch, do not become frustrated, oh Castaway,
for they are old and tired from their long journey down rivers and over seas.
Only once you have established shelter
can you go out into the wide world beyond these grey hills.
Do so stealthily or openly, that's your choice to make.

Once you have returned, you may find your shelter lying on the floor.
Do not cry threats, oh Castaway, for the wind and waves have merely
lulled the tired bones to sleep in your absence.
They will stand to attention once they realize you have returned.
You must now make like a wave, like a breath.
Go out, return in, go out, return in.
You must repeat this until you return to find tussocks squatting in wait for your appearance,
bristling with cold feeling.
Now is the time to leave, for your welcome has been out-stayed.
There is no use in bargaining with tussocks, Oh Castaway,
for they keep a tight grip on their land.

ISABELLA HADLOW

Playing Possum

Lightning lit the raindrops and sparkled on the groaning windows. The wind rattled the building, and great rolls of thunder dwarfed the 25 six- and seven-year-olds of Room 5. Nerves were stretched to the brink and very, very occasionally, a whimper was heard through the noise of the storm outside—but of course that was just the mice, Marley and Bob. No true Tikorangi kid would be scared of a measly thunderstorm.

A stormy day at school was always exhilarating—huddling together on the mat, pretending not to cower at each crack of thunder or flash of lightning, while the crazy kids stared out the inky windows, entranced by the extraordinary light show outside. It was an exciting morning by any standards, and that was before the possum came to school.

At about ten o'clock, a gust of wind threshed its way into the classroom, sweeping along with it Mr Taylor, our greying principal, and a weedy Year 6 boy named Hilton. They were both enveloped in huge raincoats and were dripping water all over the floor. Our lively Scottish teacher was frantically straightening papers and retrieving errant paper clips, but she still found the time to spare them her customary eye-roll greeting.

"Morning, class," said Mr Taylor.

We chorused in reply: "Goo-ood mo-oorning, Mis-ter Tay-lor." Some of the wittier boys added "and Hilton" to the greeting and were immediately cowed by a bone-chilling Scottish glower.

"Hilton has something to show you all. Please be quiet to avoid startling … um … it."

Hilton was clutching what looked like a furry hat wrapped in a scarf which appeared to be breathing, and a pack of un-laminated cards, grey with water damage.

Sebastien Frost yawned and fell asleep under a desk. Everyone else sat and crossed their arms and legs, whispering curiously and peering over the heads of the kids in front of them.

"Quiet," said the teacher, and so it began.

Hilton cleared his throat and fumbled with the furry bundle in his arms. It had ears! Everyone gasped.

"This is a baby possum. Her name is Charlie." Everyone gaped.

"We got Charlie when Dad shot her mum and she was left … um … left an orphan. She's probably about two months old." His voice cracked and Ahmed Smith sniggered. "You can pass her around the circle." He nearly dropped the bundle while handing it to Maddy C on his immediate right. "But please be careful, and I'm going to tell you a bit about possums."

Hilton launched into a speech about the living habits of possums. No one cared. In our community, Dad shot a possum and the dog got a feed.

There was a lot of awwww-ing from the girls and the occasional sarcastic "ew" from the boys as the ill-fated Charlie made her way around the circle, from one sweaty pair of hands to another. Someone tried to wake up Sebastien Frost, who just snorted and rolled over.

I admired the tiny human-like paws and candyfloss fur of Charlie, and laughed along when Alyssa stroked the wrong end of the possum. Someone sneezed. All was going well, but the tension in the air was almost tangible. Something had to give, and as you might expect, that "something" was Charlie.

An extra loud crack of thunder made the dainty Finn Keely scream, and launch the unfortunate Charlie across the room. I had never before, in all my significantly extensive seven years, seen anything like the chaos that ensued.

In short, the possum panicked. It landed spreadeagled on a desk and began to skitter its way across the classroom, knocking over pencil boxes and teetering dangerously across the backs of tiny plastic chairs. The girls shrieked and ran around in a panic at the thought of a wild animal being loose in their midst. We all knew possums were mostly harmless, but shrieked along anyway, a chorus of newborn banshees. Hilton dropped his cue cards. The boys ran riot, chasing the poor creature from here to kingdom-come and terrifying it still further. A certain imbecile named Petey Davis tried to grab it by the tail and swore most creatively when it scored a gash as long as my hand on his cheek. Most of us had never heard such words before, and the ones who weren't screeching like possums themselves spared a moment to giggle.

The possum clambered up a curtain and ripped down a poster. It toppled lamps and bowled over displays. It peed on the bookshelf and shredded a beanbag. Then it swung from the now empty curtain rail and let loose an earth-shattering caterwaul. Hilton, all but forgotten in the pandemonium, leapt on a desk and lunged for Charlie.

He missed.

The rain blasted its way through the now cracked window. Daniel fainted. Someone tripped over a capsized chair and sent my pencil case flying. Sebastien Frost snored on.

Eventually the heroic Scottish teacher had the equanimity to throw a ripped tea towel over the possum, and comparative silence fell. The only noises were Sebastien Frost's snoring and the simultaneous whimpers of Hilton and his wretched possum.

We surveyed the scene. The room was a tip. The bin had been overturned, papers shredded, pencils masticated. Crumpled pens oozed ink, and all smelt of possum urine and damp carpet.

Mr Taylor unfroze himself from the doorway. "I'll go and ring the cleaner." He fled.

The storm still raged outside, and it was still pounding on the windows and beating at the doors when Hilton's parents arrived. They swept in like a gale force wind, scooped up Charlie the possum and took her home. Hilton gathered his ruined cue cards and followed them, waving merrily and quite unharmed by his collision with the window—except for the large purpling bruise on his forehead. I quite think he was more wounded by the stiletto glare of the very Scottish teacher.

On the next day the sun glowed over the horizon and I wrote a story about our experience with the possum. I got a gold *Fantastic!* sticker for vivid imagination from the blatantly un-Scottish relief teacher, and a certificate in assembly. I was even allowed to walk all on my own to the Playcentre and read it to the toddlers.

The reliever didn't believe any of it, of course, but we smirked at one another and drew possums in art, because we knew the story of Charlie the Wayward Possum was true Tikorangi legend material.

SIMON BROWN

Showers

Water droplets raining down.
Everybody wears a frown.
The sun is hiding from the trees.
Instead a cold and biting breeze.

Puddles forming on the ground.
Rain on roofs, a thumping sound.
Icy liquid down my spine.
Umbrellas. None of which are mine.

Kids are jumping in the streets.
Rows of plastic, useless seats.
Wood is softened, metals rust.
Mud where there had once been dust.

Shake a tree and you'll get drenched.
Around the branch your fists were clenched.
A cloud of mist erupts through air.
I stand beneath it for a dare.

Put on my coat, put up my hood.
Can't stay inside, but wish I could.
Staring at my enemy's face,
I start my daily shower race.

It sprays into my eyes and mouth.
The wind is blowing cold and south.
Like nature's evil garden hose,
Is aimed directly up my nose.

Running, dancing, through the pain,
I think of why we need the rain.
Water plants, and grow the crops.
It's just a shame it never stops.

MACKENZIE GIBSON

From Where I Sit

My whole body is lifted from the crusted wooden planks below and shoved back down again by the denying force of gravity. Diesel fumes mix then settle, to reveal the massive tractor ruts that caused my jolty ordeal. The hardened tracks jump around in my vision as Grandad manoeuvres the truck through an over-used paddock towards the gate. The truck staggers to a halt, clunking back down through its gears, and I vault off the side of the tray wall. Fresh methane tickles my nostrils as I trudge across the hardened bog towards the gate with tiny islands of rust scattered across its metal frame. I swing it open, and the splutter and rattle of the engine slowly build into a mechanical symphony as the truck passes through. With the gate re-latched, I jog across the uneven ground, greeted by a chorus of moo's from the paddock's hungry inhabitants. Grandad's already at work, slicing the twine that had held the hay bale securely in place for our journey across the farm.

"I'll jump on," I shout to Grandad, over the rumble of the engine.

"All right, just be careful with your feet. They might not look it, but these bales are bloody heavy."

My gumboot grips the dewy tyre, rubber on rubber, and I heave myself up over the wheel arch, onto the tray. The truck rocks gently as Grandad eases off the handbrake and the dewy, pre-winter grass starts to move under me. I pull on my gloves, rip the first chunk of hay off the bale and toss it overboard. Rip, tear, toss, rip, tear, toss, I get into the familiar rhythm. Across the farmland plains the foothills of the Southern Alps, where I go hunting, loom like condescending big brothers. With the morning cloud now evaporated by the rising sun, I can see for miles, from the distant mountain ranges to the ever closer ocean horizon.

As the rising tide of cows starts to lap at the trail of hay, I realise we are about to make the turn into the next paddock, so I jump down into rather than onto softer, boggy ground. I heave the rusted gate through the thick mud oozing around my feet, and squelch it closed again after the big old diesel is clear. Instantly, a different scent hits me: the sourness of old silage and the faint tang of chemical run-off seem to swirl together, cutting through the crisp mid-morning air to form an altogether unpleasant odour. I pull my fleece over my nose and climb back onto the feed train. We meander through the paddock, the engine barely turning over, and slowly the "creek" comes into view. It is no longer the clear liquid I had seen in my childhood years, but a slow-moving concoction of chemicals. Browns, greens and blacks all swirling around in the oily mixture.

Grandad brings the truck to a slow halt. "Bloody dairy farmers," he says, slightly louder than normal, obviously directed at me. "Greedy buggers. Most of them, anyway," he adds.

"Those guys down the road must be pretty greedy then?" I suggest tentatively.

"I've seen a lot worse … ruining the bloody landscape, they are," Grandad mutters.

The truck starts to trawl forward again. A sullen scene reveals itself from behind the contour of a glistening hill, barely outside the boundary of my grandparents' farm. A paddock stripped bare to its soil, is dotted with hundreds of weak, scruffy cows. Most of them are covered in each other's faeces, and all of them are desperately searching for any last tuft of grass left in the sea of brown.

Not five years ago, I think to myself, a scene like this would have been unimaginable this side of the Kakanui river, which in itself is barely a river any more. This beautiful green landscape has been tarnished with the ever spreading rust of money-rich dairy farming. Owners sitting in big black executive leather office chairs count their return from a so-called "investment" in the dairy industry, without a thought for the returns the landscape is receiving as a result.

I toss the last chunk of hay over the fence to a particularly desperate looking cow, and sit back down on the crusted wooden planks, as good an executive chair as I'll ever need. You get a much better view from this one.

ADELAIDE PERRY

Silt Water Sirens

Resonant Venetian rock and roll
makes ripples in the water's rind.
Relax, on most days the river's kind
silt and shingle sit like stowaways
on this pirate ship of grinding
sand.

Among the colonnades of beaten bones
another man makes the one-way vow
and watches as his mortal coil
slinks into the tumult of aqueous oil
a life of hydrocarbons and pain
had little to give and little to gain
for deluded men.

So come, eat your ice cream or drink your wine
and join my friends in this narcissistic soup
for a hypothalamus of rocks and freshwater fleas
makes this little beast quite hard to please.
But don't you worry, wash away your distress.
For most days the river's kind

almost.

CHARLOTTE WILLIAMS

The Grass Isn't Greener

Insipid rays of sunlight tentatively fingered the tops of the towers, the square edges of which pierced the morning fog. This small window was the closest link we had to the outside world. Glass several inches thick protected us from an atmosphere devoid of oxygen.

"Good morning, inhabitants."

I glanced at the screen high up in a corner of the wall. Whispering in our ears. Watching over our shoulders. Right behind us. In front of us. Guiding us. Persuading us. All the time. In that calm, collected voice.

Mother handed me my ration of pills, with a few drops of water in a plastic cup.

I-ron, Pro-tein, Cal-ci-um…

We'd learnt the pill chant when we were young. Those mysterious phrases represented the capsules we swallowed every morning and evening. The capsules were distributed to those who complied with regulation.

"Limited water, probably for a week. Supplies shrunk by nearly three litres," Mother informed me, her dark eyebrows creasing into a "V". Father had injured himself at the factory the previous week, and come home earlier than his allocated time. Reduced water supply was the punishment.

Fi-bre, Vi-ta-min, Min-er-al…

The little capsules caught in my throat, and I swallowed hard. Lucky it wasn't a harsh enough crime for oxygen restrictions. I glanced up at the vents in the roof, as though expecting them to suddenly stop delivering the vital gas.

Mother noticed my glance. "Don't worry, they haven't reduced it this time," she reassured me. "I paid the rent last night. The bill is definitely increasing. I just wonder how many extra hours of work your father can take." She frowned, lining up the cups on the bench and checking again that the tap was completely turned off.

Father and Brun joined us as we left the apartment. Father carefully switched off the oxygen before he shut the door. We merged with the clusters of people queuing for the lift: two adults leading in front, two children following close behind. Always.

Once out of the lift at ground level, the inhabitants of our building herded together; and soon enough, the doors of the train latched onto the exit tube of the entranceway. The crowd wandered forward to file through the waiting doors. Once inside, I joined everyone as we stared up at the ceiling of the carriage—at the Master.

He gazed steadily down at us. Although I knew he wasn't really there, above us in the train, his watching eyes on the screen made me shiver.

The train pulled away from its stop, and he began to talk. "Greetings, inhabitants!"

"They are like sheep."

"I'm sorry, sir?"

"Imagine them as sheep. They *are* sheep."

"Well, they sure do act like sheep, all following each other, all pointing in the same direction, all wearing the same grey clothing…"

"Focus. It's a metaphor. They are sheep in the way that if you place them in a paddock and confine them to the grass within an inescapable fence, they will experience nothing else for the entirety of their lives. They will never go beyond the fence. Therefore, they cannot imagine anything beyond the paddock, beyond their own lives and experiences. And that is what maintains my society. Do you see my point?"

"Partially. But sir, how does a simple farm animal liken to an entire society of living, breathing, thinking humans?"

"Well, they are only living and breathing when I want them to, and thinking how and what I want them to do."

"How, sir?"

"The sheep are mankind, the grass is oxygen and other basic living necessities, which make the fence…"

"Ah. You, sir."

"Precisely. The restrictions placed by their leader, their master, form the fence. If I control the grass, I control the sheep and their lives. Even better, if I control the grass, I can charge for the grass. But more importantly, if I control the fence, I control the sheep's perception of the grass and the fence; I control how they think. The greatest danger is the fence. The sheep must believe in its existence, in order to stay within it."

"So is there not a physical fence, sir?"

"Oh, no. Most certainly not. That would require too much money, time and simple effort. Propaganda is the fence. Infiltrate the mind of the sheep and you have total control. And what do sheep do? Follow. They follow their master. When one sheep believes, they all believe. Unfortunately, inevitably, if one sheep has doubt, all may soon have doubt. Therefore I think you and I both know that there is only one option when a sheep misbehaves. Extermination. Quick, neat, and carefully covered up. Its cause clearly evident to the remainder of the sheep population—oxygen shortage, water limitations, whatever— as fabricated by propaganda. No questions asked. Not only will the propaganda cover up the unfortunate death, but it will prevent further doubt through threat, disguised as encouragement. See, when you own the grass, you own the sheep. You can control, threaten, reward, or eliminate, as you choose. This is one big mind game, with a heck of a price tag."

"Speaking of price, can you go over the shares again?"

JAKE PARSONS

The Oracle on the Third Floor

I plan to knock three times, but the door to the apartment swings open as I approach.

"Come in, dear, I've just been baking some bread."

Shutting the door behind me, I shuffle along a dimly lit hallway. The old woman directs me into a lounge, and reclines in a large armchair. I sit on a worn sofa which is angled towards an ancient television in the far corner of the room; a coat hanger has been bent into a makeshift aerial above it.

"This is it?" I ask.

"The one and only," the old woman replies.

"Where did you get it?"

"The shop."

"How does it work?"

"Very well, thank you."

I scowl. "I mean … I mean, what's the trick?"

"Dust the screen once a week and turn it off at the wall when you go on holiday," the lady says, using her age to be both smug and innocent. "Honey," she says to me, "you don't think you're the only one who comes here asking questions, do you?"

"No, I guess not."

"You guess right. So, why are you here? To nail the old *where do you see yourself in ten years* question in your job interview? To know if you've found your true love?"

"I'm just here to see if I will become successful. And I'd like to know how to get there."

"Another American dream. Really, my dear. Aim higher."

"To be honest," I say, "my friend told me about you. I think it's a load of bullshit."

"Do you now?" she says, raising an eyebrow. "Well then, watch this."

She fumbles with the remote, and the television flickers on. It shows nothing but static, and I look at her questioningly.

"So dear, shall we say five years into the future? I'll skip until then, otherwise we'll get all the toilet and home-alone scenes. And before you ask, details of the how and why just complicate everything. Stick to a quick snapshot, and you'll work it out."

I nod, and she taps a sequence of numbers into the remote. There is a pause as the television seems to process it.

"Have you ever … used it to look up your own future?" I ask.

"Oh, heavens no," she replies. "Why would I ever want to do that?"

Just as she is chuckling, an image appears on the screen. It's from the perspective of someone around my height, walking down a dark corridor.

"Is this … me?"

"Sure is, dear. In five years' time." She notices my look of extreme cynicism, and shrugs. "Hey, nothing's happening yet, but at least the future you is alive and awake. Just keep watching, and don't touch the remote. I think I have the right channel. …" the old woman mutters as she rises from her chair and hobbles into the kitchen.

I sit for almost a minute, watching through someone's eyes as they pace up and down.

There's nothing that shows this is the future, let alone the future me. It's just a bad quality video, and she's trying to scam me like she's scammed everybody else. I sit up and am almost out of my chair when the figure looks at a gold watch on his wrist. I compare it to my own: similar, but not quite the same. Enough to arouse my curiosity, though, so I watch as the man checks the time. It's the same time as it is right now, in the present. Which means it's either a very well thought-out scam or a live feed—and neither of those things seem likely for this old bat.

The person looks around and turns on a light which illuminates paintings, certificates and photographs in the hallway. I am paralysed when I see dozens of photographs of myself: accolades, awards and commendations with my name on them. Then a reflection in the glass of a picture frame. It's me all right. Darker and twisted, but at the same time confident and powerful.

The future me opens a doorway, walks into a richly decorated sitting room, and starts to read a book. But in the brief moment before he sits down, I glimpse something in the corner of the room. Could it be? The one and the same? Suddenly, the pieces all click into place. The question of my wealth and my success has such a simple and straightforward answer.

I rise from my chair and walk through to the kitchen, where the smell of fresh bread hangs in the air. The old woman is bent over the bench, with her back to me.

"I watched it."

"Good. Will you be successful?"

"Apparently, yes."

"Good for you." She turns around with a plate full of fresh brown bread. Half the loaf has been cut into thick slices, and the knife sits beside it. "Here, dear," she says, "try a piece, straight from the oven."

I reach for a slice of bread, then pause. "Is your TV ever wrong?" I ask her.

"Hasn't been wrong in the twenty years I've had it. Hell, that would defeat the purpose, wouldn't it?" She smiles.

I grab the bread knife and lunge at the old woman. It doesn't have much of a point, but the serrated edge makes short work of her, and within a few violent seconds the bread is soaking up a pool of blood on the floor. I wipe my hands on a tea towel and step out into the hallway and back to the lounge, where the ancient cathode ray television sits waiting.

It still shows a book, though I can't read the words. I unplug it, put the remote in my back pocket and take one final look around the dingy place. Then I lift the old thing up and heft it with both hands right out of the apartment, into the elevator, out the lobby doors and into the boot of my parked car.

A man with suspicious eyes and a confrontational stance who has followed me out from the ground floor knocks three times on the passenger-side window. I wind it down.

"I have to ask, sir, you don't happen to be stealing that there TV, do you? Looks a bit odd, is all."

I smile, and in the mirror I see the same smirking eyes of my future self. The man even steps back a little when he sees my mood.

"Oh, nothing of the sort," I say. "The old woman on the third floor, she's my aunty, you see. She gave it to me. Besides, she didn't know how to use it properly, anyway.'

ELLIOTT HUGHES

The Hoarder

In my bedroom I shelter a thousand clever little things.

I have stockpiled three pocket knives, with thirty different functions between them, which I open and close just to admire the plenitude of curved steel.

I have a flowery pen that I've taken apart and put together again too many times. The cap won't stay on any more.

In case of emergency, I keep at the ready two torches, a pair of pencil sharpeners and a clever little box given to me by a great-uncle I never really knew.

Three vintage planes, made from 100 pieces of injection-moulded polyethylene between them, hang from my ceiling and a fourth rests, half painted, on newspaper. I worked on it yesterday.

On an overloaded bookcase, I mound up old and new books whose pages I sniff like a wine taster.

My fat Bible flops in a navy-blue case that never gets zipped up. Its pages of extra discussion on disputed passages entice me into footnoted tangents on Hebrew translation.

A wood-carved figure with the head of a bee is posed to eternally salute visitors from his place on my chest of drawers. I have imagined him to be an obscure Egyptian god.

I hoard tiny lead-cast people in foam-lined boxes and repurposed egg cartons. When my friends come round, we play Warhammer on my bedroom floor.

I treasure a box of mechanical hocus-pocus hidden in gears and cogs and springs.

However, I'm a coward, so if the house were to catch fire, they're all fending for themselves.

ALA'H MUSA

Gone

When tomorrow starts without me
please
do not be sad.

Baba left in the summer that I turned sixteen. Suffocation. Is a. Powerful feeling. All I remember. Feeling was: suffocated. It was an unforgettable summer, not only because of the arranged marriage or the Syrian revolution, but also because of the heat waves hitting Syria, which accentuated the sense of entrapment that echoed within our country. As my thoughts return to the summer of 1970, I feel only suffocation—merciless, taunting and seemingly inescapable. Just like my future at the time.

The angels whispered
take my hand and leave.

Baba is still the most charismatic man I have ever known. But the verdict of the press was unconditional: *Rebel suicide proves successful on Swelih Road – Suicide car crash causes mass destruction on Syrian Streets – Learn to spot suicidal rebels, and save Syria.*

The accident Baba caused was "inarguably intentional', the officer had told Mama and me. He scanned us with a mixture of feelings: pity, disgust and confusion—but not a single drop of sympathy was painted onto his parchment skin. His reaction was reiterated by our entire village, because the magnitude of power the Government had over the Syrian Press left no room for controversy. There was a simple yet definite hierarchy that could not be challenged. The Government was God, the press were the messengers—merely the Prophets—and we were the people who absorbed every bullshit story they fed us. When the press declared Baba *a common rebel who was the country's worst enemy*, it resonated with all of Syria. My Baba. Maniac? Stupid? Selfish?

Sadness, my love, is an old friend
who flies away on the wings of time.
He does not mean to hurt you.
Simply,
he wishes to keep you company
for the time being.

"But Baba, he didn't leave!"

At night I would scream. Sadness pushed down on my chest, clawed at my skin until I surrendered. She was cunning. Determined. That I would never. Escape. Her pestilent touch. Over time, our association bred friendship, over time Sadness surpassed Mama on my familiarity scale.

Mama did not seem disconcerted by Baba's death, nor did she notice my distress. She was the most beautiful woman in the Village of Sarta and probably in the District of Al-Bab. Blonde, blue-eyed, fair skinned, she was like a prized jewel amidst a mountain of rubble. Yet, beautiful as Mama's exterior was, her heart was plagued by an incurable desire for wealth. As a child, I had stumbled upon Mama's terminal illness, concealed under a loose floorboard in our kitchen floor. Her secret embodied everything I despised, but Mama's avarice had impaired her vision: she only saw the most precious material things life could offer her. She was essentially a female replica of Uncle Nadir, Baba's younger brother.

Baba and Uncle Nadir were at complete polar opposites in the socio-politico spectrum. Uncle Nadir was a man of business, his mind tuned to financial perfection. That was him. He was the catalyst for my future.

There is a fine line that runs
in every man's heart.

The Creator had sculpted Baba's soul with kind hands. Although there was no exceptional depth to Baba's wallet, he carried a rare and beautiful form of wealth in his heart: his altruism. He had smoothed the sharp, ugly edges of what Uncle Nadir truly was, by claiming he was "fearful". Nadir was parasitic. He thrived off the hardships of those around him. He allowed others to fight the battles he was too weak for; so when his puppets fell short of victory he could advance and claim the spoils as his own. Uncle Nadir's actions were predictably always based on self-interest. On August 27th, 1970, however, Uncle Nadir got bored. He decided to make things interesting.

The hottest day of summer had dawned upon us. I had arrived home from school to find Uncle Nadir perched, as if he was royalty, on our *galsa*. Mama was seated next to him, her petite figure enveloped in a stunning gold dress that manifested her decadent principles. Her eyes did not meet mine. But then again, when had she ever truly looked at me? Mama was staring at an unfamiliar ring that encased her finger. Uncle Nadir was droning on about his day at work. The goddamn heat. Her ring finger. He continued. The ring. Her finger. As I stared longer at that beautiful golden ring, sense and realisation collapsed around my head. Uncle Nadir was no longer simply an uncle.

It divides mankind
into the fearful, the brave
but also the stupid.

Uncle Nadir continued to speak, but I was too suffocated to listen. Anger was knocking at the front door of my den of sadness. Calmness could only be summoned by thinking of Baba. He was a master with pen and paper; his palms held a promising career. But when you meddle in the complicated machinery of politics in Syria, the outcome is unpredictable. The Government owned us. Under its sovereignty we were merely pawns in the game of life, raised in fear, bred to be obedient. But Baba needed more than just fear in his life.

He yearned to meet the con-man called Hope. We all did, but few of us were brave enough to chase after him. It was futile, of course. Hope did not exist. But desperation induces outrageous action.

On March 30th, 1963, during the infamous uprising in the broken city of Aleppo, Baba's defiance had eventuated in imprisonment. On the day Baba was imprisoned Uncle Nadir said he "deserved it". That day I lost all respect for Uncle Nadir.

"Which brings me to you," he said, in a tone of authority that left no room for negotiation. "I don't see the need for you to attend school. I don't know what kind of rubbish my brother has fed you or what kind of false hope he has given you, but you've reached the age of marriage."

At least now I knew what he thought of me.

"You know Bilal, my business partner? He has asked for your hand in marriage. He is rich, comes from a good family. At least he will elevate the name of *this* damn family. The last thing we need is a woman in the workforce dragging the name of our family in the dirt behind her."

I tried to connect my eyes with Mama's. However, amid my sentence to a life of misery and control, she could only invest her attention in that *pathetic* ring. It symbolised everything she was: a pretty exterior hiding gross reality.

Do not forget my darling
to always be
brave.

"You're a coward."

Anger had taken control of my central nervous system. But Uncle Nadir would not take that kind of defiance, especially from a woman. He pulled back his hand and slapped me. He had seen an ember ignite in me; one that he recognised. The embers of Baba had to be extinguished, Uncle Nadir could not make the same mistake he had seven years earlier.

Mama finally looked up, but did not say a word. Silence was her best weapon.

I held his gaze, determined not to release a tear. I had spent so long building an emotional carapace to prevent me from appearing weak. *Be brave, always be brave.* I had been hit a thousand times in my life before—by Mama's lack of attention, by the Syrian revolution, by Baba's escape—and this hit was no different. The battle had to be won, the hierarchy had to be challenged.

"You're just like him," he said with disgust.

"Go to hell," I replied. He was too late. The fire had already spread within me.

Those who are brave
are not the fearless.
They are those who can face their fear.

That night I could not sleep. Anger, frustration and sadness had latched onto my soul. As I attempted to escape into sleep they wrapped their long black tentacles around my waist and pulled me back. To Uncle Nadir I was simply another transaction. His friend was the buyer, and I was a financial dependant that he would be released from.

Do not fear fear.
He is like you and me
his greatest angst is bravery.

Unable to live my life under Uncle Nadir's dictatorship, I decided to escape it. At least he will "elevate the name of this damned family'. Reputation is such an idle concept, but I knew that Uncle Nadir would rather die a thousand brutal deaths than have his reputation soiled. It was decided. I would ruin my stepfather's reputation. Absolutely destroy it. I pulled out the duffle bag I had packed countless times before when my anger and frustration at Mama had sent me into a fit of rage. As I zipped the bag, sadness started to tickle my heart. How empty was my life? I could pack sixteen years of life into that duffle bag and depart without a single morsel of hesitation. It added urgency to my situation only because I realised there was nothing left for me in Sarta or Al-Bab. Nothing left in all of Syria.

Money had always been Mama's greatest objective in life. Now, it was mine, too. To hurt Mama would be much simpler than to hurt Uncle Nadir. I went into the kitchen, loosened the floorboard and found the money. Mama had not gifted me with many things in life—I was unequivocally my father's daughter. It felt only right to capitalise on at least one of Mama's assets before I escaped. The green stack of paper had doubled in size since I had last seen it. I placed the money in my duffle bag and left with it, destroying Mama's kingdom of wealth.

Aware that loss of reputation had always been Uncle Nadir's greatest fear, I composed a note aimed to destroy it. As I approached the village mosque I surveyed its iron gates— the perfect backdrop for Uncle Nadir's humiliation. Leaving the note directly above the padlock, I felt like an artist painting a canvas that manifested the biggest religious and cultural insult. As I walked along the main road connecting our village to the highway of Al-Baba, I realised how perfect the set-up was. The Sheikh's wife Amena would clean the mosque gates before morning prayers. I left the note in good hands because I knew that by *duhur* the next day Amena's loud mouth would inform the entire village of what Uncle Nadir's niece had done. The note read:

> To the village of Sarta:
> I can't describe how much of a shithole this place is. It isn't even Syria's current situation, it's you—the people. Small-minded and ignorant. By the time you read this, Uncle Nadir, I'll already be on my way to a better life. The American military sounds quite appealing to me, but what do you think, Uncle Nadir? Your opinion is of utmost importance to me, so please mail me your thoughts. As for you, Mama, I can't believe you did this to Baba. It's as if you traded alabaster for a common piece of rock. Oh, and please send my apologies to Bilal. I really am sorry I couldn't attend the wedding, but I'm sure he will find another obedient wife to clean his filth and feed him.
> Lots of love— Khola xxx

> We may feel like broken mirrors.
> Although our reflections are distorted,
> we still see light shining through.
> Your life is a sacred vessel–
> live it well
> so that when it is
> time to leave
> you do so
> willingly.

Escape and I walked side-by-side through Sydney International Airport. I was finally steering my own vessel. I had eliminated the elements of drag in my life: Uncle Nadir, Mama, my village. All of it. I had thrown them all overboard, and for once I was in control. But was I a coward for escaping my fate with Uncle Nadir? Was I brave for defying a male's orders? Or was I plain stupid for flying halfway across the world to a country where I could only speak a few words of English?

galsa: Middle Eastern lounge set (couches are very uncommon)
sheikh: Islamic equivalent of a Priest
duhur: mid-day

DUNCAN MATCHETT

Song of the End

wife bicker
light flicker
drink liquor
feel sicker

i lied
she cried
both died
inside

door open
heart broken
feelings spoken
no joking

slippery slope
can't cope
no hope
tie rope

Not That Kind Of Woman

The Morris Minor whistling along the ribbonwood lane soared through a cloud of dust and loose shingle before rolling to a stop at the railway crossing. On the corner of Maori Gully and Arnold Valley Roads was a fairly modest house belonging to Ken and Margaret Allen. Their home, shadowed behind tall ferns, shrubs and the occasional fruit tree, was barely visible. Rotting fruit and the odd egg from nesting birds made it the ideal place for the weka to take shelter. Locals called it Weka Corner. Its close proximity to the railway crossing meant cars had already slowed down by the time they approached the corner, so you didn't get the roadkill you got in some parts of town. The Allens' house was looking pretty run down, with paint peeling away from the weatherboarding and the guttering just about all rotted away. The morning dew resting on the cobwebs almost illuminated their front porch. Mum said it was all signs of a bad marriage.

Mr Allen was in his sixties and Mrs Allen about twenty-something years younger. Big Ed, who ran the pub in Brunner, told me Mr Allen had packed his bags, left his former wife and kid, and taken off with Maggie. Mrs Allen was always known to the locals as Maggie. She refused to accept this, and would always correct people in a polite but firm way.

Local rumour or not, Mrs Allen didn't seem the kind of woman who would have an affair with a married man. An extremely glamorous woman, she had long red hair that met her shoulders, rose-petal cheeks, light sea-blue eyes and a very slim, elegant face. She looked as if she was ready to step into a movie set. She must have kept a close eye on what the townies wore, because she always seemed to be dressed in very modern gowns and skirts. Mum said she sewed her own clothes.

I reckon a lot of the women in town felt Mrs Allen was a threat. I had never seen her with any other woman around town. Apart from the occasional passing chat with Mum, she seemed to keep mostly to herself.

Dad ran the local garage in Brunner. Working six days a week as a mechanic—the only real one in the area—while also running the petrol station, wasn't easy. He would drive us into town to catch up with mates while he worked. Arnold Valley was a wee way out of town, so we relied on Dad to take us in.

Mrs Allen would come in to the garage a fair few times to pick up a copy of the local paper and a magazine with images of well dressed women. Me and my mates hung around the lake, skimming stones and talking about rugby and people in town. We would count the trout in the lake if we didn't have much to do. Our population was oddly dependent on the number of trout in the lake.

One day, we headed up to Dad's garage to grab some milk. As we approached, we saw the Allens' car pulled up in Dad's workshop.

Mike turned to me. "Mum's seen the Allens' car parked up by the lake a couple times now." Mike lived further round the lake, where cars parked if they didn't want to be seen. "Mum reckons she's made out the shape of a woman a couple times now. Peering through Dad's hunting binoculars."

Mr Allen was respected in town. He didn't do much work but he lived comfortably. He owned a parcel of land beside a part of the lake that was being developed by city people for weekend and holiday baches.

"You reckon?" George asked.

Mrs Allen was browsing in Dad's shop. She had a scarf over her hair and wore a sleeveless frock with red gloves. We were walking into the shop when Mrs Allen turned to us with a startled expression on her face.

"Boys! I didn't see you ... you gave me a shock," she choked.

"Sorry Maggie," chuckled George.

"*Mrs Allen*, George," she croaked. Then her eyes met mine. "Could you tell me where the matches are?" she asked, with a comfortable smile.

I grabbed a box and handed it to her. "That all, Mrs Allen?" I asked. In her basket I could see a *South Island Drivers' Atlas*, a jerry can and a pack of rubber gloves.

I was walking her over to the counter when Dad came in. "Well, Margaret, the car is good to go," he said. He walked over to the counter and started to put her items and the mechanic bill through. When she took off her gloves to pay, I realised I'd never seen Mrs Allens' hands before. They were rough. Mum reckoned rough hands were a sign of either a hard worker or a difficult life.

Mrs Allen smiled, chucked her bags into the boot of her car and took off. George and Robbie grabbed our bottles of milk while Mike and I went out to get a rugby ball from the back shed. At the doors to the shed we found the padlock on the ground. Mike turned to me, a puzzled expression on his face. We both knew Dad never left the back shed unlocked, because he kept his expensive deerstalking gear and guns out there.

I'd begun to open the door when we heard a loud crash followed by paint cans hitting the ground. I continued to open the door, and the Allens' cat darted out and shot past Mike and me. We grabbed the rugby ball, locked up the shed and headed out. Mrs Allen lived just down the road from us in Arnold Valley so it was a fair way from Dad's garage. None of us had any idea how the cat ended up in the shed.

We went down to the park to kick the ball around. The park was on the main road in and out of town. Mr Lawson lived beside the park. Willie Lawson was best mates with Robbie's dad at school. When Mr Lawson was twelve, he and my dad and Robbie's dad got into my granddad's shed and took his shotgun. While Mr Lawson was fixing a target and the gun was lying on the ground, it went off and shot Mr Lawson in the face. He was flown to Wellington to see a specialist, but he lost his sight in one eye, and ended up with a neat eye patch. As a result, Mr Lawson hated Robbie and me, and would throw vegetables at us from his back porch whenever he saw us playing at the park.

On this day, Mr Lawson had three big beefsteak tomatoes in his thick-fingered hands. He usually missed us. Robbie said his eye made it hard for him to gauge perspective. I reckoned he just had a crap arm. This time, his arm shot back before bouncing forward to release the tomatoes, and he hit Robbie square in the face. Robbie shouted at Mr Lawson but he'd already shot inside and was standing there staring at us, with a bottle of DB in his hand. Robbie set off across the road to wash his face at the Clayton's front porch tap. He was in such a hurry he didn't even turn to check for cars, and there was an ear-piercing sound as Mrs Allen burnt rubber to grind to a halt. She wound down her window and yelled at Robbie.

"You could have been killed!" she shouted.

We ran over to Robbie and Mrs Allen. Robbie was okay, but he must've got a hell of a shock. I looked at Mrs Allen as she was stepping out of her car. She'd changed her clothes and put up her hair. In her car I saw two suitcases with clothes now finding their way out—there were enough to sink a ship. Her eau de cologne was lingering around us but there was also a thick, almost heavy, crisp, bitter smell that I hadn't noticed at first.

"You boys, stay out of trouble," she called out to us, her voice quivering.

She sounded upset. I guessed it must have been the shock. She got back in her car and I saw tears rolling down her face as she drove off. In all this excitement I completely forgot to tell Mrs Allen about her cat. I turned to see if it was too late to stop her, but she had passed the Youngs' mail box—the last house in town on the road to Christchurch or the Pass. Mrs Allen hadn't told any of us she was going anywhere. We all looked at each other, confused. Dad drove past and called out to Mike and me. We jumped in the Morrie. Mike stayed at our place every other week. His dad had died in an accident a couple of years back, so Mum and Dad had him to stay, to give his mum a break.

On our way to Arnold Valley, Mike and I were talking to Dad about Mrs Allen leaving town, and about finding her cat in his shed. Dad shrugged. He said Mrs Allen had called in to get her car checked out but hadn't said she was going away.

We were coming up to the turn-off to Arnold Valley when a large flock of birds darting past blackened the sky for a second. Soon after, we were soaring through a cloud of smoke and dust again, only now it wasn't the shingle.

"Mr Allen must be having a burn off," said Dad.

The smoke got thicker the closer we got to Weka Corner. When we stopped at the railway crossing I could see fire engines and police cars at the Allens' place, and a cloud of smoke coming from their home. My stomach sank when I remembered what I'd sold Mrs Allen.

ANA MENZIES

Loneliness

I came from over the mountains, spraying forth in rays of fluorescence, billowing out across the land. As I illuminate the rolling hills beneath me with the warmth of dusk, I find him. Seated in an armchair in a small cottage on the edge of the world, he is achingly familiar, and I know exactly what to expect as I walk through the door. His soul is warm and dry like toasted bread. Like a light layer of margarine, I reach in and spread myself. Its taste is Forsakenness, and it runs through his veins as acid. Although I leave a bitter taste on his tongue, he sighs as I touch him. I am a balm, I am a friend. I caress his soul as the last light of day fades. I am as intimate to him as he is to me, for I have lived within him for decades.

I emerge in the form of a tear, roll down a weathered cheek, slide through the chasms carved from living. The moment I hit the floor, I am gone. Off again. I never rest. As I am speeding away for the thousandth time, I admire him, for he does not wallow. He is nothing, and I mean that in the kindest way, really. It makes his suffering easier. It is better to think you are being forgotten when you know that you were never worth anything in the first place. Isn't it? With all those I visit, and those who inevitably I will meet again, I would rather have someone who is empty. Those who allow me to drag them into the mud never resurface. My job is hard enough without having to plaster myself over souls. Did you think you need a mouth to scream? Tomorrow this man will wake. He will eat, wash, and at sunset I will visit him in his armchair. I will be greeted as an old friend, and for a second I can forget what I came to do.

Next is a woman. Ah, it is nice to see a new face. I wonder if she will become a regular. I have millions of those. Arriving beside her feet in a twirl of tulle, I take a moment to catch my (metaphorical) breath. Whiteness coats her like icing sugar. A fine dusting covers everything she touches—her dress, her ribbons, her bridesmaids. I bathe for a while in this joy. That covers everything, too. Slabs of it hang from hairpins and chunks stick between teeth like remnants of an engagement dinner. I tarry; not for too long, though. I can sense that, even under all that blinding lace, a black heart cannot be hidden. I pounce, crouch on it, run my fingers over its faceted surface. It doesn't seem to refract the light around it, but absorbs everything. A piece of coal in an ivory world. For a moment I allow myself to wait, then I clamp down. My claws sink into a soft soul. It parts like damp sand beneath toes. As I sit there, in the velveteen darkness, she tenses around me. I am a moment, I am her greatest fear. You do not love him, I whisper. Right there, on that tragically beautiful soul, I begin to grow. Roots twist, crystals erupt from branches and dangle like forbidden fruit. They hang by shiny strings and each contains one word: Alone.

Afterwards, there is the swimming pool inside the teenager. Waves slop messily against the sides, emotions ready to overflow. Unstable little things, adolescents. So messy, so passionate, so afraid. There are bars on the windows. More to keep things from getting out than in, I think. But then again, I could be wrong. It has been millennia since I was young. She is surrounded by friends, by laughter, but nevertheless I will engulf her. The water drains, and a barren landscape appears. Sand emerging from the deep works its way to the surface. Scalding grains push through cracks in her soul, drawing the water hungrily into them. Her sanctuary is being invaded, foreign fire inhaling the cool liquid. The heat bubbles up and scorches her throat. Her mouth freezes in mid laugh, suddenly dry and parched, because inside her a desert now fills that swimming pool. Stumbling through it in a few days, she will arrive at realisation. She will stumble over it, half buried in the sand. Companionless. Through the haze and the confusion she will reach for it, dust off the last shreds of hope. How that emotion clings to things, I have no idea. Almost as if it had a life of its own, you could say. Well, you wouldn't be that far off.

A neatly trimmed lawn. Perfect roses sway in an imaginary breeze. See it? No? Then I will show you. Nothing is perfect. Those roses, with creamy crisp petals and shiny thorns, are a lie. The girl where it exists lives in a broken body in a broken home. I hide within her as the words slap her face and leave handprints on her soul. But it is not here that I show myself. I arrive in silence, and it is in silence that my presence is most felt. The gaps in the thin morning air between sleeping and yelling. The clatter of cutlery bouncing off barriers at the dining table. The rumbling purr that cushions the tension of a morning school run. I alight on her lawn, a razor sharp idea slicing through these moments. Unloved, abandoned. In the silence when the breeze begins to tug persistently at her clothes, I look away. I will always choose my purest form to visit her. Alighting, I beat my white wings, faster and faster. The ground shakes, petals fall like rain. However, when I next return, they will each be back in their place, adjusted and glossy. Did I mention how much it hurts? Because it does. Looking at her hurts. I feel keenly at these moments how small she is. She is still growing, and it makes things so much more difficult, even though there is less space for me to fill. I long to hold her, to comfort her, but that is not my job. Feelings are fleeting and fast, and I have places to be.

Emotions are tangible things, you know. They are my friends. I have walked with them in the dusty corridors between souls. We do not often have the luxury to stop and chat, but we acknowledge each other's presence as we dance together in the hearts of souls. Humans are blind. They blunder around waiting for words to explain how they feel. One day, when humanity has fallen (believe me, that day will come, I am counting on it) we shall have time to talk. To compare the souls we have handled, lifted, broken, carried away. Perhaps in those discussions *you* may come up. An example, a punch line, a regret. It could be an honour, or maybe the lucky ones are those who are never mentioned.

The truth is, I try to forget you. I try to bury the pain I cause. There is a brief moment though, as I am flying away from your rose garden, or your swimming pool, or your toasted bread soul. I will wonder, *am I destroying you?* Or is this thin glue of breakfast spread all that is holding you together?

Remember, I am a beast of your own making. I only come when called. Please be kind. I have hurt everyone who reached out to me. In a way, I am my own monster. I have walked across every sky that has ever existed. Seen all the colours imaginable. I prey on you in your lowest hour. I inject into you one of the strongest fears of human nature. To be an outcast, to have nobody to love or be loved by. I have touched, spread, drowned, and clawed every soul in existence. I have done all this, alone. I guess you could say it is the loneliest job in the world.

ERIN DONOHUE

When Your Therapist Asks Why You're Crying

Blame the tightening choke-hold anxiety.
Your sparking wall socket of a heart and
the helium balloons tied around your stomach.

Blame how anxiety works 24/7, how it never
takes a holiday. How it never lets you
breathe without tasting blood.

Blame the anorexia and how
she invites herself to every meal. Blame how she can
always find room for herself at the table,
no matter how many loved ones surround you;
no matter how little you have eaten that week;
no matter how many times you
have heard the words,
please, just eat something.

Blame how hospital admissions
are used as scare tactics.
Blame how there are scarier things in your head.
Like the thought of gaining weight or
the phrase, *you look better now.*

Blame the depression and how there's nothing else
to say but *blame the depression*. How it can leave you wondering
if your words have dried up like
blood around a small wound.
How it hollows you out until having a
shower means completing
your to-do list.

Blame everything
that's ever made you cry.

When your therapist asks you why
you're crying, ask her,
why not?

CHARLOTTE BOYLE

Counting Waves

I lie wrapped in insomnia
like a second blanket
that makes the bed just a little too warm.

In the quiet my eyelashes
beat against each other
like a clock ticking to remind me
that I really should be asleep by now.

My duvet envelops the silence
a vacuum of sound
somehow still loud enough to keep me awake.

The fishhook curls of my hair
stretch across the pillow trying
to catch dreams without bait.

When I take a breath
the darkness moves in
and out like a black ocean.

Counting the seconds between each wave,
I don't remember when they stop.

GEMMA MCLEOD

Anorexia in Twelve Words

The blue mist
the glazed eyes

frosted over with ice
in July

SYDNEY HARDY

Control and Free Fall

Control

It was a beautiful spring day, too hot according to most places, but in Texas 85° Fahrenheit was normal. I sat up in bed with the sun streaming through the window and rubbed my sunken eyes. My skin felt more slack than it had a few months earlier, and this gave me a flicker of joy as I realised it had something to do with malnourishment. Turning to look at my pillow, and feeling the bones of my spine as I did so, I noticed a few strands of hair left behind. There were always strands of hair wherever I went: strands on my jacket, strands on my pillow, strands on the couch.

The sun illuminated every detail and every speck of dust in one half of the room. Like a sleepy cat, it stretched as far as it could, but it could not reach me. The golden streaks seemed like fools' gold; I could see its light but not feel its warmth.

First, pushing back the covers, I brought up my knees until I could clumsily slide them over the side of the bed and stand, with a bit of effort. I walked over to the door, which held a full-length mirror, and the mirror held me.

With trepidation about what lay beneath, I stripped off. First my shirt, then my pj pants, which hung so loosely now, until I stood stark naked in front of the mirror. I stretched my torso and grabbed at my ribs, trying to count them. I then stood straight on and looked at my thighs, literally my biggest insecurity. Feet together, thighs apart. My inner thighs looked further apart than yesterday, but still touched at one small point near the top. No matter how much I wanted them to part, the two fatter bits reached for each other like star-crossed lovers always managing to hold hands, if only just.

Looking up again, I turned sideways, took a deep breath and released it, letting my stomach muscles completely relax and push out as far as they could. I paused in this position, refusing to take in the next breath until I'd completely analyzed every facet of fat. At last I allowed myself to breathe again, and studied how far out my stomach would go as I breathed. And finally I sucked in to see what that looked like today. My mid-section, like my thighs, looked a little smaller than the day before, but still did not reach my goal.

I mentally steeled myself for my next task of the morning, the scales. These measured my self-worth and had the ability to bring great and indescribable joy, yet also the ability to send me spiralling down into a silent pit of self-loathing and depression. On bad days the depression felt almost as heavy as my weight, and the scales reminded me just how much that was. I would soon find out what kind of day I would have today.

I crept silently down the hallway, the carpet cushioning my steps. Heel to toe, heel to toe, I slowly approached my mother's room, where the bathroom held the scales which held my self-worth, and she shouldn't know that I had stood there or she'd know that illness had found me again. She was upstairs drinking coffee, enjoying the fools' gold streams that jumped through the window. These days she only added cream to her coffee instead of cream and sugar, in an attempt to be healthier.

Now I had almost reached the bathroom, with its cold floor, a wide mirror and the scales of self-worth. I held my breath and stepped onto the scales, refusing to look down as their small squeaky complaint told me they had measured my happiness. For a full minute I stood like that—erect, sucking in, and head refusing to look down—to gather courage and strength. At last I couldn't bear the wait any longer. I looked down, feeling the adrenalin rush I would never become accustomed to, and looked at the number that meant so much on the tiny screen: 0.6 pounds less than the day before, 5.4 pounds to my goal weight.

I stepped off, relieved and happy, and immediately rushed back to my room to look in the mirror some more. I was nearly 10 pounds down from where I started, but no amount would ever be enough. Relaxed again, I put on my clothes and began to brush my hair, pleased when it continued to fall out. Soon I would walk upstairs and eat the same thing I ate every morning, an egg with salt on it, 70 calories. Then I would go on my phone and enter 70 under the breakfast section of the MyFitnessPal app.

As I ate my egg, sunny-side-up, I turned towards the sunlight swinging through the window and smiled at the warmth slowly seeping into my body. My skin took it in like a starving man at a Thanksgiving dinner. It seemed to be wishing that my body was capable of photosynthesis, converting solar rays into food to replenish my weakened limbs and never more than half full stomach. I smiled, because I knew that it couldn't. For the first time I felt as if I had control, and yet deep inside, I knew my smile was as empty as my stomach, for what really held control was the scales which sat unwittingly in the bathroom with the cold tiles and the wide mirror, completely oblivious to its tyrannical control over my life.

Free Fall

We called our home an upside-down house because the living room and kitchen were upstairs while the three small bedrooms were downstairs. I sat at the dining room table, sipping coffee and cream and enjoying the sunlight knocking on the window for permission to climb through and light up my day.

It was a beautiful day—a Saturday, thank goodness. No work. I worried when I was at work, because my dearest daughter was either at school or at home by herself, locked inside her room like some kind of vampire. Yes, I prefer to be at home, so I can be there if she needs me, and where I can keep an eye on her. I don't know what's wrong, but my gut tells me there's definitely something going on.

My gut always knows when something is up with my girl, like the time she wanted to go to a party but I said no because my gut said to hold her back, and it ended up getting busted by the police. I think it's just part of being a mother.

I checked the time, hoping she'd be up soon. Seven-thirty. She normally gets up instinctively around eight or eight-thirty, because that's the time she wakes for school. The night before, I had woken up at five a.m., sweating and anxious for no apparent reason. I crept along the hallway to her room to check that she was all right, pushed open the door as slowly and quietly as I could, and despite a few squeaks, peeked in. To my relief she was okay. There she lay on her bed in a troubled sleep, twitching every once in a while. Comforted, I returned to my bed and slept a little more soundly.

Now the coffee smelled nice and seemed to beg me to relax, and while I did my best to oblige, I could never completely let go. I was always so worried for her. I felt like a secret agent trying to find out what's going on, without being pushy or cruel. How could I make her understand that I love her no matter what, that my love is completely unconditional? She would not understand how loved she is, until she learns to love herself, which I know because I struggled with that in my teen years and still struggle today. ... Have I passed this issue on to her? Is her struggle my fault? Did I make the wrong decision about her father or did I wait too long to make it? All these questions spun through my head faster than the speed of light, orbiting around my head space but always returning to the forefront of my mind. I was always scared. Always. I felt as though she was slipping out of my grip like sand through a sieve and the farther away she got from me the less I could help her. She was so out of control, it was as if she was in free fall, and I was powerless to catch her and hold her still.

I jump as the stairs alert me that my daughter is on her way up. I know her morning routine so well that I can predict exactly what she'll do and in what order she'll do it. Up the stairs she comes, and says "Good morning, Mum" with a sad smile that doesn't reach her eyes. She gives me a kiss on the cheek and pads toward the kitchen to cook an egg sunny-side-up. I watch intently as she turns on the stove and places a pan on top, then sprays some Pam before flitting to the fridge to pull out the egg. One egg has about 70 calories, as she has informed me ... I wish she would just eat twenty to make me feel better. Her legs, which have lost their baby-fat, look weak and frail. My gaze reluctantly travels up to her arms to study how flat the muscle is. I hate this, examining her secretly every morning, checking to see if she's lost weight. Silently I beg her to eat a doughnut or something with so many calories it could fill a starving child with one bite. I've begun to despise the saying, "there are starving children in Africa who would eat that." It may be true, but there's a starving child in my house who won't.

As she sits down next to me, holding her egg on a small plate in one bony hand and the salt shaker in the other, she looks into the sunlight and smiles. It's an empty smile and I yearn to fill it with my love, but she won't accept it. As she sits there, I look at her warm brown eyes. I love the way they shine in the sunlight, and no matter how her body changes, those eyes will always stay the same. I watch the light land softly on her skin, softly so she doesn't shatter, and wish that her skin could perform photosynthesis and convert the sunlight into food to replenish her fragile body and soul. My vision suddenly blurred because I knew that it couldn't, and I cried because I knew that she was too far gone to let me help, and I didn't know if I would ever get her back.

ALICE PARK

Mother

I used to think
my mother knew
everything

that as soon as she rose
she knew that
we all loved her
to pieces

and that she knew we loved her
when she climbed that mountain
every day at dawn to
break her back

and when she sewed those clothes
every day at night
when even candlelight was reluctant
to ruin her fingers

and especially when she went to sleep
next to a cold side
where a photograph lay
and there was no light to blow out
no cheek to kiss
no warm fingers to grasp
I used to think
she knew

but maybe
all she remembered
was the skinny baby crying
in the middle of the night
and didn't want to sleep with her
because her bed was too cold
because she couldn't read
and couldn't help with homework
because she couldn't buy him a house
and maybe all she
remembered
was her own heart breaking
breaking

Revert, Return or Restart?

Gaming is my escape from a miserable so-called life. Life used to be enjoyable when families were happy and at peace, but now I sit here, pathetically slouched in my computer chair, clicking the world away. Walls bang, glass smashes, voices scream, it's all that ever happens in this wretched household.

I login my Equinox18 account and to my surprise the screen flashes the recurring word ERROR in assorted colours. Stupid computer, it always goes on ahead and beats itself up when I need it most. Just before I attempt to spam every single key, it pauses, then transitions to a picture of me with five little words: *Zeke, Restart? Yes or No.* What does this mean? What. . . .

Everything starts to disappear. I pivot around as the door vanishes into thin air, as do all the contents of my room. Black, it's all black. Confused, I slowly lurk around the room, trying to maintain consciousness. Don't faint. Don't faint. Don't faint. A bright, incandescent ray of light appears, revealing a colossal wooden door with a giant spray-painted question mark on its surface. I hesitate, then twist the knob and exert force onto the door.

This is it? Another dark room, containing nothing but a pathetic plastic table. Resting on it are three round red buttons each labelled with thick white text:

REVERT   RETURN   RESTART

What does this all mean? As I turn to leave the room, a powerful voice fills my mind with all the possibilities the buttons can offer.

Revert forces my parents to tolerate one another like they used to. Return takes me back to my normal life without changes. But Restart. . .

Restart fixes everything: it allows my parents to pair with the ones they really loved, the ones that weren't each other, the ones that grant them happiness, the ones that have threatened my very existence.

Simple. That's all it should be. Just a press of a button and POOF, lives are changed, people are happy. Why is it so difficult to do? I inhale deeply and close my eyes, fearing what could happen, and then I press the button.

Echoes of voices dart around my head and my hands start to fade as the virus crawls along my arm, deleting every cell in its path. Tears stream down my cheeks as I realise what is the recurring problem for my parents: me. I gasp one last time before my entire body disappears again into darkness.

The sound of footsteps nears. I hear a faint noise. Laughter? A hand touches me. My eyes crack open to reveal two silhouettes back-lit in the doorway. My parents.

"Happy birthday, Zeke!"

OLIVIA MAXWELL

Seams

There were holes in my skin,
just little ones
needle pricks not big enough to bleed

She saw them,
the girl with the swishy hair,
and she fed them with whispers … *who brings a whole tomato for lunch?*
That's so weird …
and one morning I woke up
to find my nails chewed around the edges,
and the pinpricks turned to gashes

Out of the gashes tumbled sounds,
murmurs of fears and spluttered secrets that said too much
and he heard them,
the boy with the newest chucks,
… are you reading?!? Don't you have an ipod? Geek …
and one morning I stopped bringing books to school

His words were pulling at my edges,
tugging at jagged pieces of skin
before I could stitch them hurriedly up, and pretend
to like Taylor-Swift-And-Lipstick
like everybody else
and as the ache spread,
the world poured in through the open wounds:
magazines and billboards
… you are not normal…
lyrics and music videos
… you are not good enough …
flooding my insides with something soot-coloured and heavy,
and some mornings I don't eat breakfast
any more

the world is growing blurry
and the wounds have all reached out
to each other, seams now,
running right down my sides
and slowly coming un-stitched;
and maybe no one can tell
that I am leaking out through the gaps

but
she understands,
the girl with the thoughtful face,
... hey, you like Tolkien too, right? Want to
go see the new Hobbit movie, maybe ...?
and sometimes it only takes the tiniest bit of thread
to start sewing a seam back together.

CELINE KAO

Symptom Girl

She asked me if she was the problem girl. She had given
up on smearing concealer on her wrists, industrial strength
would not cut it any more.
A dose of sleeping pills, with a side of
cheap vodka for dinner on gourmet
Tuesdays, she had been
surviving by way of things that would slowly kill her, an
ironic cause of life on her life certificate.
Her void looked a lot like the ghost I was
chained to, the one who wished for flight down a seven storey
building, three winters ago.

I watched her bleed as people lived
between parallel lines: beside each other, but never
touching; screens tinted their favourite shade of alone.
Humanity weeps in the corner at
this era, where ego lies in the thumbs of the
populace, and compassion drowns
in the wake of illness.
Paper-thin friendships crushed her
bones, and she band-aided her
skin with cigarettes, until she was nothing more than smoke and
mirrors; but she was not the only one with broken insides.
I answered that she was not the problem girl, but the
symptom girl.

AMY CRERAR

They Call Me Ink

I've never really been like the others. A grain of salt in a sea of pepper, that's me. I apologise for the vagueness of my description but it is true that I know only my name and what is reflected in the mirror: tall, lean, pale-skinned, mousy brown hair, hollow blue eyes, rigid smile, slender fingers. I'm not particularly sure why I look like this. I've been told my birth mother was as plump as a pumpkin and my father, a rather muscly frame. *I told you I'm unusual.*

If you're curious as to the rest of my family—my sisters and my brothers—all I can tell you is that they're busy doing something somewhere. Walking tightropes over the Grand Canyon perhaps, directing the latest sci-fi, training to be the next great musician. These are just a few probabilities, and I guess I prefer to assume I'm correct. Sounds rather hypocritical considering my answers to questions usually oppose the very idea of *correct*. My mother's friend enjoys emphasising the wrongness of my introversion. My unknowingness of myself does appear a little abnormal, but when it comes to my imagination—well I like to think I have control.

The doors were daunting. Three metres high, three metres wide but somehow small enough to encourage a little shoulder rubbing. I stood on the steps, my ears tingling with the melody of voices. My first class of the semester consisted of the generic and most deeply despised "introductions".

"Jenny. I'm here because biochemistry and atomic structures are absolutely fascinating. I come from a family of seven, two sisters, two brothers, myself and my parents. Oh, nine if you count my two cats Margo and Jelly Worm."

Why she would name a cat after the squiggly member of Party Mix, I don't know. My introduction on the other hand, went a little differently.

"Chrissy… 18, Lancaster."

"Is that all?" they would ask, and I would nod. I had nothing to hide, but I also had nothing to show. I didn't usually have much to show for myself. I turned up at the odd social occasion and decided that was good enough. My presence has never been regarded as anything other than unimportant.

March 1990, my fourth birthday. The first and last time I celebrated the glorious day of departing my mother's womb. I never did embrace the excitement. December 2005, my first and my last school disco. July 2009, the first time I embraced an art class and perhaps more particularly, the first day I was marked with significance.

It was out of frustration really. The emptiness was no longer empty, the isolation no longer isolated, as every thought was returned to the outer layer of my skin. The tingle of the ballpoint gently released the screams from within, words and thoughts too violent, too dangerous to be left on the inside. It started with an *abandoned* and ended with a teardrop leaking from my wrist bone. It progressed to an *unacknowledged* and a stream of salty ignorance.

"Why on earth is there a waterfall hanging from your wrist?" my mother would protest.

"Not hanging but merely sitting, mother," I would say. "I give entitlement for this lovely stream to make its home on my skin."

It made sense to none other than myself. Counselling, therapy, hour-long consultations—why endure such vulnerability? Why have your heart strings pulled upon so vigorously by a complete stranger? I think I'd much rather spill a little ink than spill a little heart.

I'm not looking for an intervention, if that's what you're thinking. I refuse to let these little spills of ink suggest anything other than my internal frustration. Unlike an ordinary eighteen-year-old girl, I am an honest portrayal. What you see is literally what you get; teardrops, waterfalls, riverbanks overflowing with words, phrases and sentences. Terminal loneliness restricts any desire for approval. They can snicker, they can joke, they can question, but I am 100% oblivious and 110% unaffected.

Oblivious, I sketch below a weepy tree on the upper side of my thigh. The branches hang loose, as does my body, spread spiritless across my bedspread. It's 2 a.m. and my brain won't stop ticking. The jelly worm cat, the introductions, the way my father spoke to me over the dinner table. The few too many drinks, the headaches, the nausea and the toilet bowl. I am left pining at the table on my left for the most impenetrable pen of them all. My head rush-rushing with demonic adrenalin as I recount the past few minutes, days, months, years.

It all comes flooding back, as does the waterfall draped from my wrist bone. Foster home after foster home, *No mama* after *No papa,* a mouthful of derision after a slap in the face; how I'd wished they would taste their words before they spat them at me. My mind races furiously, as does the black against my skin. I scribble myself into oblivion.

With a bang on my door and a twitch of an eyelid, the day is alive. Stretching over to peel back my blinds, I am made aware of the bleakness that is May the 4th. Rain is bucketing down and condensation embraces the windows like a sweaty snail trail. *Disgusting.* With much hesitation, my groaning body rises to a seated position. A figure stands at the foot of my bed, a bit like a soldier with his shoulders tensed. My (current) father. Ohhh, wonderful.

"Good morning, Ink," he murmurs.

I give him a nod, too dreary to function below the neck.

"Clean it up, okay," he replies, closing the door behind him.

Clean what up, I think to myself; looking around at my perfectly tidy surroundings. My books are ordered alphabetically and my desk is a lot cleaner than his. I continue to look around, clueless, until my eyes meet the mess on my bed, and more specifically, the girl seated in the middle. The mess he was referring to was *me.*

"Oh my god," I whisper, in a panicky state.

Oh my god. What is this? And this? *And this*?! I ask as I point to various body parts. The stains scream agony, humiliation, distress. The blackness that cloaks most of my body also marks my linen like a big, blotchy stamp.

I step furiously out of the mess that is my bed, but am left with the mess that is Chrissy. Examining the imagery only makes me all the more angered: ISOLATION drawn in bold down my thigh. I close my eyes but it won't go away. The painkillers, the alcohol had most certainly worked before, but the ink had never been so overpowering. The very sight of it ran shivers down my spine … the smell of it too toxic to inhale.

My body stood still in the middle of the room, numb to the unmoving presence of my past. With a choir of wasps making their home in my head, I race downstairs to the emptiness of the lounge. My foster parents have left for work, and a part of me can't help but resent their absence.... *they always leave me. Why?* For once, the ink that marks my skin doesn't stop the tears from marking my cheeks as I search the room for some kind of solace. I rush around uncontrollably longing for something; something to erase hopelessness.

"ERASE, WILL YOU! ERASE!" I scream as I kick open the front door.

Furious, I release every tension with one high-pitched yelp. I hurdle over the sloppy garden fencing and the mushy mounds of grass. I kick the rose-red pansies, perfectly aligned in height order. I tilt my head back to the sky and feel a torrent of rain rush down my neck. I stand, still and saturated, my fingernails digging furiously into my thighs.

"Mummy! Look!" I know I'm manic when I hear a voice in the back of my mind, overpowered by the relentless choir of buzzing insects. "Mummy! Mummy!" it repeats.

Confused, I slowly and reluctantly open one eyelid at a time to reveal a little girl standing on the opposite side of the road. A pink umbrella and a pair of gumboots. She's pointing at something: a lonely figure, a lonely body dripping with something more than stormy moisture.

Ink.

The ink is trickling, the ink is running, the ink is flowing from my body. Each drip competing with the next in a race to reach the soil. Surprise sits unmistakeably on my face as my pupils dilate to mammoth proportions. Examining my discoloration is a daunting process, like a solution to a word problem: here, and then gone with the swipe of an eraser. To my surprise the wasps have dulled their melody and my mind becomes a little freer from obsession.

I don't understand why I am experiencing such relief. I should be angered at the ink dripping from my arms and trickling to my toes. I should be enraged at my incompleteness, but instead I find myself embracing a new kind of freeness. How could this possibly be, I wonder, stunned at the sight of my ink-naked body. My white shirt hugs my skin as did once the ink. Five freckles kiss my wrist as did once the stream of salty ignorance. The scribbles on my skin—so liberating at the time but such a visible reminder of the pain, the agony, the abandonment—are they out of my system, or as present as ever?

For the first time, standing in the mushy mess beneath me, I feel what it is to have a choice. Perhaps the starkness of my skin offers a new kind of expression. Perhaps there is, and this is the next step away from the internal frustration and the external reminder. They call me "ink" but I am not always ink. I am Chrissy.

Perhaps healing is something more than what I have made it.

PATRICIA GOH

The Essence of Conformity

The music blared shrilly. Explosions of high frequency sound waves resonated within her body, the beat of the music making her feel as if she had a heart abnormality. But that wasn't all that was bugging her. A strange but familiar feeling was also growing inside her. It started from her heart, crept to the very ends of her limbs, and crawled around her neck until it decided to rest at the back of her brain. All of a sudden she found it hard to breathe. Was it affecting her lungs too? Maybe it was just the dress. *Oh don't be ridiculous. Your dress isn't that tight,* said a voice somewhere deep inside her. "I know, I know," she said aloud, though she clearly disagreed. She decided to leave it at that for now; she couldn't think of any other reason.

Three young ladies around her age in pretty, formal dresses circled and pranced about. They looked rather silly, grooving to the music, swaying their hips and waving their arms in the air as if they were having a good time—though she was sure they weren't. They just had to pretend they were. Everyone had been anticipating this since the beginning of time. There were boys there, too, some with girls sitting on their laps whispering and giggling, locked in each other's embrace. How lovingly they gazed at each other! Some of the girls looked so bad, it was almost as if they had dunked their heads in a bowl of flour, and applied their lipstick with a paintbrush. She cringed; she couldn't bear to face them, seated at the sides of the hall, at small round tables with food and drink, being careful not to crease their fancy laced dresses and nicely ironed blouses, or smudge their make-up.

"Maybe I should have brought a partner," she murmured, regretting her decision to go solo. Then, at the very least, she could pretend that she wasn't alone.

So there she sat, watching the dancers on the stage while she assumed the role of an audience, giggling when they flailed their arms as they lost their balance in those unfamiliar "dancing shoes". It really was very entertaining.

"Hey! Want to come and dance?" said a girl smiling down at her.

"Sure. Why not?"

A lively upbeat tune had leapt out of the large loudspeakers. She sprang to her feet ... but others suddenly surrounded the girl and, chattering excitedly, pushed and shoved her (now visibly embarrassed) to the centre of the hall, smirking and gesturing at one of the guys at the side to come and join her. *Never mind then*, she thought, slumping back onto her seat. She didn't *have* to go.

A while later, more girls and their partners waltzed to the centre of the hall. She could have sworn that she hadn't seen some of them before! They looked quite different—and yet, frighteningly similar. They had the same dull black dresses that looked so alike, as if bought from the same shop. Those who had straight hair had made theirs curly, and those with curly hair made theirs straight. They were nearly beyond recognition. Everyone wore high heels, including the tall ones—as if they needed the extra height. The boys were no different, in the same black suits as everyone else. What else were they to wear?

More and more people were joining the party. Even the ones who sat at the sides, like ragdolls on a shelf, started to move forward. Now she was alone at the sideline, a shadow whose presence was neither seen nor felt. She knew what she had to do. Slowly, she got off her seat. After a few sips of iced fruit punch to help clear her thoughts, she walked nervously to the centre of the hall. It was only when she was two feet away that she noticed they were dancing in circles like tribeswomen around a campfire—well, several campfires. She couldn't believe it. What a silly thing to do! The flurry of dresses and girls twirling around laughing reminded her so much of the children's game "Ring A Ring a Rosie" except that they weren't sweet, innocent little girls. Everyone belonged to a circle—even the ragdolls formed their own circle. Everyone had their place, everyone but her.

Perhaps she should just turn back. She didn't belong here, she never had. It was more fun watching them. She wasn't party-dance material. But then a strange urge to join in compelled her to stay. She tried to will herself to walk away, to walk back to the chair of shame and stuff herself with more blue cheese and crackers, and more fruit punch. But for some reason she was rooted to the floor—as if her toes were screwed to the wooden boards and her body was a statue. She started to panic. What was happening to her? *Never mind*, she thought, trying to calm herself down, *I'll just join in somehow.* As she inched forward, the music seemed to go faster and faster. People seemed oblivious of her. She shuffled closer to a group. They didn't budge.

"Hi! Can I join you guys?" No reply. Perhaps the music was too loud. "Hey!" She was sure they could hear her, for she was shouting into their ears and even tapped one of the girls on the shoulder. It was clearly a mistake. How she wished she could just disappear beneath the floorboards. She felt like a castaway clinging on for dear life in a dark sea of people, bumping her about, waves of hair slapping her face over and over again, party lights flashing like lightning, the music beating as loud as thunder. …

There was no one left to join at the sides. She wanted to leave; she felt so uncomfortable it was almost unbearable. Warm blood rushed to her flushed face, now burning with shame. She wanted to cry. What if people saw her? What would they think of her? She glanced at the teachers chatting at the end of the hall. What would *they* think of her? *Who cares what they think?* said the little voice inside her. *You're not having fun here.*

Taking a big breath, she pushed herself out of the stampede, at the risk of getting trampled to death. At last she could breathe! She sat back down, in the same spot as before—no longer as warm as she left it. Even the cushioned seat had grown cold as if to suggest that it wasn't her spot any more. But she sat there anyway. She needed to rest. She would never attend a social like this again. Never.

Soon it was time to go. The bus painfully dragged its tyres along the gravel road and heaved a sigh as it drew to a halt. She sat alone. She didn't know anyone, anyway, but it was all right. She just wanted to be alone.

"Hey, it was good night eh? Did you have fun?"

Fun? Hah! Not even close. But that *yeah* was the correct answer. She couldn't say no. It would've seemed weird of her to do so, especially when everyone else seemed to be having such a wonderful time. Whatever! She didn't want to think about that now. She didn't want to think of anything.

She sighed. At least she had tried. Nothing really mattered any more. The formal was finally over. She crossed her legs and closed her eyes, and listened to the humming of the engine as the bus crawled home.

Six Feet Over

I am not well
That line is not poetry
Illness is not romance or performance art
or a journey or a slap on the wrist from the gods
It's just a gradual changing of preferences
a fading photo, a ripping dress, a beast shedding its skin
and revealing weak flesh beneath

I now prefer to wear materials that are difficult to rip
cotton coffins, shackles of lace, clothes that are tighter than my lungs
Balloons pushing against an ivory cage
at a birthday party on the wrong day for the convenience of others
with a new family heirloom that doesn't suit my curves

A homeless man told me
that my smile was the flesh of a peach
wet with spit and sharp to the tongue
Something unexpected under a velvet exterior
then like Moses he parted the sea of cars
and sent me home with a desire for cigarettes and sherbet

I told him that there's a moment during the process of drowning
where water becomes air
and that air is sweeter than your first kiss,
(outside a dance hall
while your friends sway inside
with whiskied breath and laddered stockings
where boys' fingers attempt to climb to forbidden fruit
trying to take the apple
without the gods noticing)

Today I took my emergency number
folded it into a paper crane
and set sail on a saccharine sea
spitting sugar pills from my mouth
like teeth knocked loose in a fight
between two halves of an uneven heart

November 8th

"I – I'm sorry, Matt."

"Why are you sorry? What's happened?"

"I can't do this any more."

"W … what?"

"We're through. I'm breaking up with you."

"What? Why?"

"I can't handle you any more, you're always just a huge downer, it's like you think all your problems are the only ones that matter, and that I don't at all. We can't work out any more. Besides, I'm going to Spain for a month. Do you really think our high school relationship could survive that?" She laughed, then hesitated and dropped her eyes. "Sorry."

That *sorry* meant nothing at all to me. I walked away slowly, my legs carrying themselves. I sat down on a park bench and stared up, tears trickling down my face. She said I was too much of a downer. That's true, I guess. I have a problem, which began at the start of this year, when I first got checked out.

"I'm sorry, but Matthew has a problem," the doctor had said, his words soft yet dry. "Matthew is suffering from schizophrenia. However, at this stage the effects are mild, and it shouldn't affect his life if he takes medication." He picked up a bottle of pills and shook it.

It shouldn't affect his life. I remember those words to this day. That doctor had helped. He'd quietened the voices that plagued my mind day in, day out. They were still there, but so quiet I couldn't hear them half the time. I felt nothing but goodwill towards him, and after that appointment I visited him every Sunday until two months ago, when during a dinner, he choked on a fishbone. The restaurant was sued, but it didn't matter. That's when everything began to spiral out of control.

I began to feel weaker, the voices grew louder, I kept forgetting to take my pills, and my work ethic began to slip. I was a pretty smart kid, but after the doctor died, I couldn't think. My mind couldn't seem to work out problems I could've done in my sleep before. The psychologist I was seeing put it down to depression, on top of everything else. He was probably right. I'd been failing school. Now my girlfriend was gone I didn't see the point of living.

"Hey, Matty, what's up?" A spark ran through my brain. I recognized that voice. "Get up! What's wrong?" Arthur, my oldest friend, sounded genuinely concerned. I looked up and saw his homemade bracelet sparkling in the sun.

"Don't worry, Arthur," I sniffed, wiping my face.

"I *am* worrying. Did Jess break up with you?" He grimaced. "It's all right man, I'm here for you."

I chuckle. "You always could read me like a book."

"Let me take you home."

The walk home never felt so long. There was absolute silence between us. Arthur didn't know what to say and I—well, I just didn't feel like trying. I walked slowly inside. Arthur asked if I wanted him to stay and I politely declined, saying I'd rather be alone. I crashed on the couch and stared at the ceiling. As tears filled my vision I blinked, and the cream painted ceiling was suddenly a dull pinky-grey. I stood up, and realised how little space I had. The lounge had changed into a small pink room with tendrils snaking down from ceiling to floor. I was trapped, stuck in this place. I knew I must be dreaming, and pinched myself to escape from this prison, but it didn't work. Through the tendrils the walls looked like uncooked mince, and I saw other prisoners in the same position as I was. They all looked similar to me, with only small differences of hair, eyes or nose.

"Anyone home?"

Hearing the call, I was suddenly back in the lounge, panting, staring through the window at the apartment opposite. I had no idea how stressed I had been, how fast my heart had been pumping and how much my brain had hurt.

"I am," I called in response to my mother. "Listen, I'm super tired so I'm going to bed."

"Good idea. It's school tomorrow, remember!"

* * *

In the morning I wait outside the gate for Arthur, as always. I wonder if I should even go to school, seeing how terrible I feel. I don't want anyone to have to see me looking so bad. I contemplate turning back, but hear footsteps running towards me.

Arthur's usual energy and aura of happiness are still evident as he flies around the corner. "'Sup, dude," he calls. "You ready?"

"Do I look not ready? I've been waiting here for almost ten minutes. Where've you been?" I grin half-heartedly, returning my phone to my pocket.

"Let's go then, ass." Arthur lightly punches my arm, and his bracelet jangles as we begin our walk to the subway.

"Well, I gotta run to band practice. See ya in English, Matty!" Arthur calls, sprinting away as soon as we pass through the school gates.

It's early, and I, well, having no other friends to walk with, I wander through the empty hallways, staring at the floor.

"Hey." A quiet voice echoes, and I look up to see my ex-girlfriend.

"Jess!" I cry. "What are you …"

"I came to see you, Matt. I felt we left on a bad note, and wanted to fix some things." She walks towards me, her footsteps loud in the seemingly abandoned halls, and I realise it's more than Jess. It's lots of her, at least twenty. I smile at them all; all of them have different expressions. One in the centre is grinning, one to the right is angry, one is crying and another is laughing; I love them all so much.

"Jess," I whisper as they all fall on top of me, hands clasping around my neck, each and every one of them putting pressure on my windpipe. I choke, unable to breathe but so happy. They all merge into one Jess, who's crying, laughing and angry; she has a seemingly infinite range of emotions, her fingers still pressuring my windpipe.

"I love you, Matt," she coos seductively. "I can't wait to see you again."

Smiling, I struggle to force air into my lungs. Black dots dance before my eyes, and I realise I'm in danger of dying. I mustn't die like this, I need to push her away but with numbness once again flowing through my body I try to scream, but croak instead. I try to yell "Jess you're choking me!" but I can't, and she won't stop. Her tears drip into my eyes and mix with my own, and I can't breathe ….

"Hello?" I call out. "Hello?" The hallway is still empty, and my greeting echoes. "Jess?" I call again, hoping for some response. I wonder where she's gone. She just tried to kill me, and then she just up and left.

"Why are you on the floor?"

The lazy tone of the school counsellor makes me tilt my head.

"B-because Jess, my ex-girlfriend, she was here, and she was choking me and there were lots of her then not lots, and she was crying and so was I, and I passed out," I gabbled, panting at the effort.

"While I admit you do have bruises on your neck and you do seem very upset, I don't think it was Jess, Matthew."

"Who was it then?"

"I don't know; but I do know that Jess left for Spain this morning, with the rest of the Spanish students."

"B-but she was here a-and–"

"Just don't worry about it. Can you stand? Let's get you to home room. Then at lunch you can head over to my office and we'll talk about it."

I still don't see how she could be here and on a plane to Spain. I know I saw her, and I don't know why she wasn't there. Maybe she didn't go on the trip. Maybe she has a secret twin. I don't know, and I don't understand. Maybe I'll be able to get it when I'm at home; I'll just have to wait out the school day.

We're waiting at the station. Arthur is explaining a movie idea he's had, some sci-fi crap, nothing super special.

"And so … like … the space cruiser has been absolutely destroyed by this little drone, and everyone's researching how something so small can do something so big, and … and then this kid figures it out and …"

He's going off on a tangent, and I lose him in my thoughts. About Jess, about the doctor, about work, about everything like that. Suddenly I hear a squeal, and in Arthur's place I see a giant fish-faced thing with whiskers and a gaping jaw filled with rows upon rows of teeth. Screaming, I push at it and a cracking sound fills the station as the train pulls itself over the monster that took Arthur's place, and everyone stares at me, mouths wide open.

I freeze at the sight of what is left of my best friend. His spine is like a spear sticking out of his skin, his face so destroyed you could barely tell who it was. His brain spills across the tracks and blood flows from every orifice of his body. All I recognise is his homemade bracelet sparkling in the sun.

"I'm sorry!" I call out to Arthur but he doesn't respond. "I'm sorry, Arthur I'm sorry! Come back up, we have to go to school. It's dangerous on the tracks, man!" Crying helplessly, I run to Arthur's mutilated corpse and hold him in my arms. "Wake up man, we have English homework, get up, you have to write your essay!" A sob escapes my throat every second word, my tears flow over him. "Get up, please, please get up," I whisper, but arms suddenly grab me and try to pull me away.

I fight off the arms and run, my arms and legs pumping me away from the station as fast as I can, pushing people out of my way. I run into someone, fall down, and look up to see a policeman. I quickly apologise then sprint away, running blind, thinking only of two people—Arthur and Jess, rushing through my head, over and over again.

Desperation leads me to a tall building stretching high above my head. It bears the logo of Brodrick Industries, my father's company. I run inside, unsure of what I want to do in there. The blank faces of the employees are nothing to me as I push them aside and get into the open elevator, slamming the button for the highest floor. The elevator lifts, and I'm completely alone for this brief period of time. I decide what I want to do, why I came here, and I prepare to run again when the door opens.

The top floor is filled with offices and people doing their work. Fatigue no longer affects me. I run up the stairs to the roof of the building. My heart thumps in my ears, and I know what I came up here to do. I step onto the edge, and then hesitate. Do I really want to die?

"Matthew, what are you doing?" My brain recognises a familiar voice. The doctor. He is here? I look around but can't see him anywhere. "Why are you even thinking about it? Remember our time together? Did that mean nothing?"

I shake my head in frustration. "You don't understand; everything's bad now you're gone!"

"Don't go yet Matthew. You still have so much time, things will get better!"

"No, they won't, they never will! There's only one solution for me. Then everyone will be happier, and everything will be better!"

Silence. The blowing of the wind is all I hear.

"Hey, kid! Stop, don't jump!" I turn around and see my father's assistant standing there, concern in his eyes. "There's no need to jump, man!"

I blink. I don't think he can even remember my name. I can't remember his. Nothing comes to mind except Arthur and Jess, Arthur and Jess, Arthur and Jess. Sadness grips me like an iron fist, and I swallow hard before speaking.

"I'm sorry."

The building flies past as I fall. Floor after floor. It should be a quick escape, but time slows and it feels like eternity is giving me time to brood on my thoughts. About what my doctor had told me. Would he have wanted this? My dad's assistant screams at me, but the noise is muted. What if this isn't real? What if this part is all in my head? That is just as likely as this actually happening. Maybe none of this has happened, and when I hit the ground I'll wake up in a green field, with Arthur next to me and Jess holding my hand.

PRU RHYND

Tanka

but in your last breath
you will find it, the knowing
moments of peace you
fly, ballon in liberty
with peace you cease to exist

Ballon: in ballet, the ability to appear effortlessly suspended while performing a jump.

LARA WATSON

"Hello, our name is…"

We were playing elevator tag the first time I remember meeting them. Shrieking, shrieking, pressing buttons in between belly laughs, shrieking. He was tucked in my shirt pocket, trying so hard to breathe. She had these flecks in her irises, as if someone had tie-dyed her eyes. I too had no breath left. It was so ethereal, yes, it was that limbo between the tip of the mountain and the sky, arms wide. We held so many secrets between our teeth and when the frown in the power suit strode onto the lift we leapt off, as if we had been scalded.

I saw them again on various occasions, leaping from shoulder to shoulder, catching bonfires and late night whispers in a butterfly net, stringing them back through my ears as I slept. I tried to paint them, to put them into poetry, to press them like flowers, but they could not be contained. He had spiky sundial hair and a mad grin; I'd always look for her in magazines (but to no avail) and in finger-to-fence rhythms, oh I'd always look.

Almost, almost as good as I should have done.

Soon enough centimetres sprouted from hairlines, matchstick dents littered doorframes, and we began to water ordinary dirt and bulbs of balcony dreams. I saw honey but tasted rust. The very valleys we knew like a religion dissolved as our bones, like oaks, grew rings. His name was seen only in the newspaper amongst the flotsam and jetsam of monotony, she was merely the vandalism of all grown-up blooming under park benches. They were an aroma. The thought-behind-eyelids-elephant in the room.

Over time, their names became no more than placid totem poles next to my letterbox, an embossed certificate on my CV. Some called me eccentric, said I had crooked teeth, wondered why my palms were tough from old blisters. They whispered, "Bitter… childish… foolhardy."

One day, though, I replied: "Yes, but perhaps I am also wild hearted" and there they were, tangled in my hair, dancing like wee tears on my eyelashes. The children and their mothers said *Weird* and loped off, pursing their lips as if *they* had been scalded.

I have come to know now, that macabre and micawber only vary by a few letters and I think that phonetics was trying to tell me to let fear slip-slide into awe, because I got out my looking glass again. Unearthing yellow treasure maps and crumpled movie tickets, I smiled. I smiled a raw and magic smile!

I knew they would stay awhile when my fingernails started growing back. When the picture frames were crooked I let them be, because I could see footprints all over them.

But I began to forget what a yoyo was built for, and I climbed so high I thought I didn't need air. Everywhere I went, I cajoled her into coming with me, I prodded him into collarbone holes, and sometimes I forgot to introduce them. I think, that's when whimsical adventure descended into wistful misadventure. Because even in this to-and-fro declaration of living I can still say that misery *always* loves company. And, I was trying so hard.

They left the next day.

I was in an elevator some time later, going downwards, all nicely pressed, plum pencil skirt, glum. They came tearing in, two gangly kids, jeans ripped at the knees, four hands hanging on to their torn fabric, squealing, squealing and pushing an array of floor numbers as they clutched their stomachs. I started pressing buttons, (they gave me the strangest looks) and just as I stood there chuckling, I heard the slightest whisper, a tinkle of a sound: "Hello, our name is…"

"I know who are happiness, I know."

"Oh! Well, that's that then. I'll be seeing you around yeah?"

"Yeah."

After that the elevator was empty. I rested my head against the wall as I waited for it to go up and down, up and down, and up and down again.

CELINE KAO

Ce Que Nous Avons Fait

Inspired by Sarah Kay's *Questions and Answers, in No Particular Order*

I don't remember the number any more, but it was on Primrose Street.
When was I prettiest in your eyes?
Fifteen minutes, but you kept saying twenty-two.
Would you like a napkin to clean that up?
Orchid. That night lingered in my room until infinity faded.
How far did we run?
Blue, but blue like daybreak, not the jazz of night.
Why were you counting my breaths?
All the times you yelled at me for adding more salt.
When was our last kiss?
Three p.m. lust.
Did you feel the months stacking into seasons?
Spaghetti bolognese, with one too many tomatoes.
Could you tell by how many inches of rain there were?
Vignettes of yesterday etched into the wall.
What did you do after we said goodbye?
Yes, but my dreams escape me like water evaporating.
What could I have done instead?
Nothing, because it was never meant to last anyway.

TIERNEY REARDON

Stories the Bus Won't Wait For

The clouds are her breath in the early daylight hours;
thundercloud blue shadows paint each street she haunts.
on the days she forgets her gloves
her fingertips go numb.

She lets conspiracies collect in her mind,
feeds them like mice
with the crumbs in her pockets.

The rippling tide of the sun creases her skin;
a gold cross hangs around her throat –
a sign that she searches for signs.

Perched on benches in bus shelters
she has stories for anyone willing to listen
about the price of milk, dull joint pain
rosebushes and predictions of rain.

She tells her son over the faint static of the phone
about the newspaper boy this morning;
the paper he threw landed in a puddle by the doorstep.
the words had blurred, nearly beyond recognition
but she could just about make them out.

Sometimes she can spend hours at a time
counting the rings on her fingers,
counting the loose change in her coat pockets,
counting stories she hasn't yet told,
counting birds and cars and people.

counting down.
She knows its only a matter of time
until the phone static begins to fill her bones.

ISABELLA HADLOW

Caroline is Not like Me

Since I cannot tell you about the butterfly boy, I will instead discuss Caroline with you, the girl I am inclined to wish did not exist.

Caroline is not like me. She is stubborn, true, and brave. She is also clever, but where we really differ is here: Caroline prefers to exist Somewhere Else, whereas I am firmly anchored in the Real World. She cares for her friends, of course, but this does not redeem her; they too exist solely Somewhere Else.

Caroline is really the opposite of me. She has more confidence than I ever will. She is not afraid to pass judgement and will stand up and speak for her passions as vehemently as a politician speaks against his. I wish I could do this, too, but it seems hard—and perhaps it's just because Caroline lives in her head and we lowly beings are really only rarely graced with her undivided presence.

Caroline and I are not alike. She does not look in the mirror other than to check the mess of dark heaping curls. It is not the fear of hating the golden-edged chocolate eyes or chestnut skin that repels her. It is because she wants to see only what is not there, rather than what can be seen from the outside—which is to say, what is not there and maybe shouldn't ever be.

Caroline and I share few similarities. She is quiet until the time comes to enter the Aceldama of reality and fight for herself. Caroline's world is very much private (some people think she is strange, and they laugh behind their hands), but it is also her kingdom—a Queen puts her people before herself—and if she told and said not to tell, everyone would listen. Caroline has a soft voice, but when she speaks, even the wind outside stops to listen.

Caroline is not like me. She is a great inventor of words—autumness, liquifidity, watersent. Where one does not exist, Caroline will create another to fill its little empty void, whereas I prefer to experiment with the millions that are already there. Every word has a colour, a texture and a shape, and so Caroline draws them (but only *her* words—the others do not belong to her, and she cannot ensnare them). She does not draw her people, though. Never; for if Caroline can draw them, anyone could, and they would not be hers, and they would not be worth fighting for. You can take them, but you can't ever have them, she thinks.

Caroline has never been a friend of mine, as she dissects the world far too much and seems to love the idea of non-existence. She, like me, wonders why we need oxygen to breathe, but also thinks that time and motion and life are impossible, which is a repulsive thought. She questions what should not, in my opinion, be questioned, and so I am almost scared of Caroline and her incredible, insane wonderment at the things that Just Are and Should Be.

No, Caroline is not like me. While I know her well, Caroline and her secret world are not like me, and she will never be my friend.

There is more to say about Caroline, but I am short on words and time (and of course, time is money but far more valuable) so I will leave you with what you should really remember about Caroline: Caroline is Not Like Me—or, indeed, perhaps I am not like her—and no one else can see her.

PHOEBE LIVINGSTON

This Perfect Storm

Louise knew very well how addicts felt when trying to come clean. There was maybe half a day of feeling on top of the world, thinking you'd saved yourself and made a fantastic leap forward in your growth as a person. This was quickly followed by the first pangs. A weaker woman would have crumpled here. Many did. It was like an old and familiar lover leaning on a doorway and smiling in that exact way you loved to see, the jersey that was too ratty for polite company but so soft and comfortable that you couldn't bear to part with it. So much easier to return to the old pattern than venture out into the unknown. Louise had fallen at this step before. Cell phones and the internet made it harder to ignore what she wanted.

Then there was something like a second wind, wherein you've defeated the first pangs and feel at your very strongest. You've tempered yourself like steel, and you're now a better person to face the world.

And then there was anywhere between a few days and a few weeks of detox, which made the previous steps seem rather delusional. This could involve horrible physical upset, and heroin addicts coming clean have been known to lose a dozen kilos at this stage in a messy process best not discussed. Others have blackouts or become feverish. Alcoholics get both aggressive and desperate. Smokers get the shakes and the sweats. Because at this point, your body is resisting the removal of something it honestly thinks it needs. It's the same as going off water, or so your system thinks.

And, if you succeed in that stage and you don't relapse or die, you face a lifetime of desperately wanting to go back. But hey, you managed to come clean. You can get a little positive buzz out of that, which is good, because you'll learn quickly that the world outside of your vice sucked as much now as it did before. Heck, that was probably what triggered your use of the vice in the first place.

Louise was at the beginning of the second-to-last stage. She was sitting on her couch, looking at his name on her contacts list. If she deleted it, she'd be getting a step further than she had in the past. If she kept it, she'd know that she would never get away.

It was always hard, when he was in a good mood, to want to leave. He was perfect, really; his smile was the infectious kind that made you feel like you were sharing a private joke. He played the piano and wrote songs just for her. When they were separated for any length of time he'd greet her at the airport by picking her up into the kind of warm hug that made her feel there was nothing the world could do to her that he couldn't fix.

Gods, when she'd met him, it had been amazing. They'd been working on a movie together, and he'd come to her caravan after a day's shooting to get acquainted with his co-star. A few hours in, she'd unloaded everything off her chest and he was messing around pretending to know how to taste wine while she ate KFC and made fun of their script.

She'd been dating someone else at the time, but frankly she hadn't cared, not from the moment they'd had to do a slow-dancing scene for the movie, and whatever had happened had felt real. The first few weeks had been great. Benjamin—no one ever shortened it to Ben, because it felt wrong in their mouths. He was Benjamin Noble, no commoner, and he was all heart.

Red-carpet affairs were never so scary with him by her side. His perfect confidence made him forward-going but never arrogant; and that, coupled with his relaxed and easy charm, had instantly made him interviewers' fodder and Louise's best friend.

His acting abilities were flawless, on screen and off. Off screen especially, and the only time he ever dropped his perfect act of being the most lovable star to ever have wandered from Westminster into Hollywood, was when he was at home.

Louise could never, in hindsight, put her finger on the moment he'd dropped that mask. It had probably happened gradually, the darkness inside him cutting bands through the light that shone from his smile. At times she even doubted which one was really him, good or evil, because he blurred the lines between them with frightening ease that could only make you wonder.

She had once heard that if you dropped a frog into boiling water, it would struggle and try to escape, but that if you initially put it in a nice temperature of water and heated it gradually, the frog would die without struggling once. Maybe it wasn't true and maybe it wasn't supposed to teach any kind of lesson except the proper care and disposal of frogs, but she now thought she knew how the poor amphibian felt.

He was cruel and cold, Benjamin. It wasn't that he hit her. She would have walked away immediately if he had. No, instead he cut her down. He made sure she knew full well that she and everyone else bar him was worthless. He had this peculiar way of *knowing* people, staring into what made them *them*, and from afar she'd seen him use it to get what he wanted in a way that made people happy to give it to him.

He never directly insulted her, never directly dug away from under her. Instead, he just slowly siphoned off her self-worth with that trademark confidence, worked on hollowing out the warm feeling that her chest used to have when he was around.

After maybe a year of her alternately tolerating and adoring Benjamin, he swept in with a brilliant smile on his face, kissed her soundly and took her on holiday. And Louise thought, *he really does love me.*

Two weeks later she had one of the worst anxiety attacks of her life because he'd said to her in that perfect, elegant voice of his, "Frankly, Louise, of the many things you have ever told me, I think this might be the most ridiculous. And I emphasise that it has a lot of competition in that everything that comes out of your mouth is best ignored."

She had just told him that their dear pet cockatoo had died and that she wanted to hold a little funeral and bury him in the lawn. But it wasn't what he said, or any part of the situation. A bird was just a bird. It was that, when her lips went a little slack and her eyes closed a little in shock and pain, a harsh, coldly amused grin curled the corners of his mouth, a funhouse mirror reflection of his usual warm smile. He enjoyed messing with her, and that was what made it a crushing blow.

Some people can excuse the behaviour of their significant other by saying that they didn't realise what they were doing. But Benjamin knew, and he revelled in it.

She'd turned her eyes from him, feeling a surge of emotion claw like heartburn up her chest, and her breath came out as a rough gasp. In their bedroom, with the door closed, she'd tried to fight hyperventilation and mostly failed until she fell asleep.

And yet, when she woke up, he'd cooked them both a lovely meal and told her about his day as if she hadn't just sobbed for half an hour and slept for three. It felt almost apologetic, but there was no apology. There were only those intelligent brown eyes, surveying her as if he were trying to look into her chest and see how much of her heart was left.

His kind gesture made her feel that she really had been over-reacting, that mourning the loss of her pet was a little overboard, and she was just easily offended. Being caught on her wrong foot like that had messed with her head, but she was used to it now. She just accepted that she was wrong and he was right. The random bursts of affection didn't stop, though, especially in public where it looked good. He seemed a perfect romantic, and under that there was a sociopath. A well-restrained one.

Calling foul would never work. He was a media darling. It had already been conclusively proven in Hollywood that any accusations made about beloved celebrities would quickly slip into the futile recesses of people complaining on the Internet.

She did love Benjamin, or more accurately she loved the face of Benjamin that swept her off her feet at random times and seemed as if he genuinely adored her. He did it just often enough that she would weather the bad times with his perfect image in her head, and this was probably intentional, because no one knew people like Benjamin Noble knew people.

Louise had now gone a day without making contact with him. She'd gone through the first three stages of withdrawal and was living in her old flat to see it through. Step one of coming clean was to throw out your stash, and his radiant smile and ability to cut like a knife through her thoughts would bring her back every time if she'd stay around to see it.

She'd felt very good for the first few hours, just as expected, and then felt miserable and beaten down. However, she'd pushed through that to feel her current indecision and fear about the momentous decision she'd be making if she forged ahead with her plan to cut him out.

Her thumb hovered over his name, pondering deletion of or answering his text from earlier, which just said WHERE ARE YOU? Deliberately no emotion either way, to keep her guessing.

She tried to focus her mind on disbelieving that smile, but it always shifted, in her head. She wanted to focus on the cruelty in his eyes, the way his teeth looked weirdly sharp when his lips twisted like that, but the coldness of his features always shifted to the warmth of their first kiss with chicken grease on her hands, or the laughter of watching her learn to ski with poor results, or the way he bit his bottom lip a little while composing at the piano as he thought of her. When he was in one of his good moods, she was never happier.

She'd broken the back of an addiction before; nothing serious, just smoking a few years ago once she'd grown out of a teenage habit. The five steps had passed by, textbook-style. And yet now, a couple of years later, her fingers still twitched to her pocket and she missed it dearly. She may have given it up for her health, but at the same time, between the rough fits of coughing, she'd enjoyed the cool relief.

And what waited for her, after Benjamin? Being his girlfriend was the only reason she was famous, and she had no notable life skills outside of acting, to which no one paid attention anyway. Her parents adored him and he was a fixture among her friends. She wasn't a person outside of being his partner. Life with him as her vice was bad, but she realised that life without him would be so much harder to bear for so many different reasons.

She replied to his text.

She couldn't help it; she had nothing else to offer herself. In her mind, just how he wanted it, he would always be perfect, and perfectly hard to shake off.

LEAH DODD

Under Your Skin

You are an echo
a sea salt moment, a silk memory
a smile trapped like suns sealed
in jars you are not the skin,
bones or colour of your hair

You are a ghost
that echoes of gold and green like
a tea-stained shirt, or the leftover smoke
that hangs thick in the sky after
coloured lights die away

You are not filled
with soft desires and
you do not breathe honey clouds
into languid skies as
you did one olive summer,

(You are nearly empty)
that knowing look dancing
across your face like old dreams
as you scattered stars
into the sky like ashes

You let midnight in
let it stain your palms
as it soaked through in
full and now the sun is fading,
the fog of dusk clearing, and

You are an echo
a sea salt moment, a silk memory
a sealed sun waiting for the storm
to set free the ghosts
under your skin

LARA WATSON

Stick Figure Absolute

There was nothing half-hearted about this one. In fact, she was one of the most wholesome, wholehearted souls I'd ever met. She was a Give Way sign. A Give Way sign at a retching intersection. One of those people that left postcards in your letterbox on a Sunday afternoon. She was absolute. A stained-glass window, unstained by the dust of exhaustion. Her personality was a join-the-dot precipice, arms flung wide atop the cliff-face. She liked to fill teabags with the good things she'd done. You'd get a jar of breaths for your birthday, and this was not unusual. She would give, and give, and give, and give and give.

This language, this faith, was unwoven by the hourglass, though. Her spine shrugged white lines along the road, her eyes were "GO". Her fingers shook as her head nodded, her eyelashes both damp and dry. She was haphazard. A tugboat for the Titanic. She had as many thoughts as there were things on her floor. You'd get a wet pillow in the morning, when dew had crept in through the window. She would give, and they would take, and take, and take.

She was a doormat; we saw her begin to become dormant. Only we were to blame, we knew. She was absolute, absolute in every shade, her only mistake was letting us scramble to get pieces of her. We were greed. We were a different kind of absolute. Stick figure absolute. She was vivacious and we were viscous. So easily we stole what she was so eager to lend. She would have given you a buttonhole for every day of the week, but you delighted in the whole garden. I drank her nights, let her vertebrae contort to the geometry of my whims. I didn't see it as a sin, until she was empty.

Impaled On Trust

The tent sat like a sanctuary, its canvas wings flapping slightly in time to the wind. Further ahead of her, he had taken his knives out and was fidgeting with them. It was fascinating to watch. The knives flickered through his fingers as quick as lightning and it was impossible to tell how many he held in his hands at any one time. Once she thought she saw several leave his grip.

He parted the dense fabric of the tent. Tiered metal benches lined the walls, all facing a massive circle of sawdust, which was surrounded by planks of wood. The planks were painted with blues, reds, yellows and swirls of burgundy. The target was propped against a bench on the far side of the marquee, standing out, but not flashy. She traced her hands along it and was unable to find any piece of the smooth surface it once must have been. She stood with her back against the board, and waited.

He looked at her in a peculiar way. "This is extremely dangerous, you know."

"I know."

"You could die."

"Yep."

He sighed. "You have a serious problem."

He braced himself and all he had to do was flick his wrist for the blurs to start rushing past. She flinched slightly when the first one went in. She could feel the air shifting around her, and the sheer force the knife gave off when it hit the wood. She had expected the sound to be more of a plink, but it was a definite thud, hearty and sure. To her surprise, she loved it. She loved the rush and the sweet taste of adrenalin in her mouth. Perhaps she did have a problem. God knows how many she already had, burdened in her mind. Except little of that mattered now. Not moving was what mattered. When she was standing against the target, life was incredibly simple. Stand still or die.

There was no sound. He had stopped. When she realized that his hands were empty, it seemed wrong somehow. She took a step forward and turned to face the target. The knives were arranged in a perfect outline of her body, with splinters scattered at her feet. She reached out and touched the cold metal. A few weeks ago she would have thought of it as an ally, a way out. Not any more.

He watched as she pulled all the knives out and gathered them between her small fists. Gingerly she passed them to him, and he still watched her, with a million silent questions. Instead of attempting to answer any of them, she stuck out her hand and he could see the tiniest of smiles on her face. He shook her hand, enveloping it with support, comfort and confusion.

"Again?"

Kayak Camp

"Time to get up." A loud, deep voice echoes around the camp.

There is a rustle, rustle, as the tent is shaken to wake us. *As if we hadn't been woken by the loud voice.* Reaching my hand out, I hope my torch will still be beside the cardboard-like roll I have barely slept on. The light blinds us like deer in headlights.

"Are you serious? It's 6.30 already? I don't want to get up," my mate groans, sinking back into her sleeping bag.

Wheeeeew, it's the last day. That's the only thing getting me through. I give up caring, and head to breakfast in my pyjamas. Of course, with the boys in charge there's toast everywhere. I down it and head off to find my half-wet thermals and collect my wetsuit from the line.

Kitted out with our bright red lifejackets, yellow helmets and spray skirts, we hit the van and take the short trip to the river. The usually talkative ride is full of silence and resting heads. Everyone is dreading the next hour. The van halts on the grass verge. Through frosted windows and morning mist I can barely see the rushing, roaring river. *Oh what fun this will be.* No one moves. Just sits. Still. Then the call from the teacher, "Right everyone out," and the door slides open. We flood out, standing around while the usual two get all of the kayaks off. This is terrible. *It's cold, I can't feel my fingers, it's early, I'm tired, and now I have to get wet.*

I quit whining. It has to be done, and I know there's a hot shower waiting for me at the other end. I grab the end of the bright red piece of plastic that I'm putting all of my faith in, and drag it towards the water, arriving next to my mate. I am met by a seriously unimpressed look, to imply she's feeling about as enthusiastic as I am.

"Right, today's the last day. You've done all of your practising and you know what to expect. Now it's time to do it. This is what will count for your final grade." As she talks, I attempt to stretch the stiff, soaking, spray skirt around the lip of the kayak. It flings off, not co-operating. Even the simple task of getting into the water seems painful today. I am physically and mentally exhausted. My once lively outlook is as dead as a doornail. My body aches, every movement a constant reminder of the challenging past couple of days. Seeing my fading patience, the teacher lends a hand.

I throw my weight forward, to propel myself from the edge of the riverbank and into the water. *Plop.* The front of my kayak dips and a freezing splash sends a shiver down my spine. This triggers my only goal for today. **Do not fall in**.

I drop my paddle down, focusing on the technique I've been taught. Usually I would ditch it and do it my way, but it's better to do it properly since we're being assessed. I speed up the strokes in the hope of getting to the front of the pack. Kidding myself that if I go first and fall in, everyone will see, and race to help. Scooting in between two other kayaks, I raft up for a debrief before the first rapid.

"Right. Everyone try to keep as far right of this rapid as possible. This is the tamest bit, but you don't want to get too close to the bank. Remember your strokes and S turns across the eddy. Eilish, in this rapid you need to roll and be buddy-rolled for your achieved mark."

Really? I have to go upside down underwater and rely on someone else to come and save me. Man, I hate kayaking.

Approaching the rapid, I keep as close to the instructor as possible. The closer she is the less time it will take for her to rescue me. Nerves kick in, my heart beating like a drum as I see what I'm in for. The waves slashing into the sharp bend stain the wall of the bank. I drift closer and closer to the rapid. Knowing that it is unavoidable, I go for it, paddling as fast as I have ever paddled before, creating a swift transition from tranquil water to turbulent tide. The overpowering current picks me up and heads me for the corner. *Great, exactly what I was trying to avoid.* With my arms rotating like a propeller, I keep my eyes on the calmer waters ahead. The waves plunge. Up. And down. Up. And down. My kayak follows, jolting to their rhythm.

I know now's the time to make my move. In the split second before the next towering rise, I thrust my hips firmly to the right, dig my paddle into the water and drag it against the strong flow to direct my kayak to calmer waters in preparation for the roll. I reach the side, somewhat relieved, but know this is just the beginning. I call "Ready?" to the instructor, who's cruising cool as a cucumber down the rapid. She responds with a thumbs up.

Wrapping my arms around the hull, I hug it as tightly as possible. Hunched over, I keep my nose on the front of the kayak. I lean my body to the right to become unbalanced. Plunging into the ice-cold water, I go into instant shock. I thought I knew what coldness was but, boy, was I wrong. There was no preparation for this. The raging river sucks out any warmth left in me. The demand for oxygen and the overwhelming temperature send me into a panic. I forget everything I have been taught: *relax, clear your head, tap slowly three times*. I drag my arms out from the kayak and back to the hull, fast and forcibly. BANG. BANG. BANG. I give the code: I'm ready to be saved.

Waiting, I sink into a mental haze. The silence is deafening. My head spins. I am upside down and the swift swell is sweeping me with it. I squeeze my eyes shut to block out what's happening. I hold my breath for what seems like eternity, wondering if she's coming to save me and at what point I wet-exit. What is she doing? Did she hear my code? Did I do it too fast? I bargain with myself: three more seconds. Three … two—my count is interrupted by the jolt of the instructor's kayak colliding with mine as she comes to the rescue. Her arms stretch over the lip of the kayak. There is a tug, and in one sharp movement I rotate fully and erupt from the water. Gasping for breath, I am unable to see, as my soaked hair has flopped down over my face. Flipping back my hair, I suck the crisp air in and out, in and out. My breath looks like I smoke a hundred a day. My skin burns on renewed contact with the howling wind. Drips slithering down my back send my body into shivers. I squirm as the pool of water that has filled my kayak itches between my thermals. Ironically, this is all delightful in comparison to what I have just experienced.

As my breathing returns to normal, it's a few seconds before I realise what she has said. "Good job. Smooth roll. You pass."

Between chattering teeth, I manage "thanks" and a smile. *Wahoo! I've done it.* Relief flows through me like a beautiful blue river. I am ecstatic. The self-doubt has dissolved and so has my bad mood. The sleepless night spent worrying about making the grade now seems silly. I now know I was in safe hands and there was nothing to be scared of. The hard work in the last four days has paid off.

Rite of Passage

Getting your driver's licence is a rite of passage, a passing into freedom. Freedom to drive by yourself on a nifty scooter. *Beep beep!* Suddenly you are also the chauffeur for the family who have taken up shrieking spontaneously every time you reach a roundabout or major intersection. You can now drive your parents home from scintillating social functions where they struggle to maintain the necessary sobriety to be a legal co-driver. It's one of the most important teen-ranking procedures … more divisive than having (or not having) a partner for the ball. This process is a glorious level playing field, one any 1st XV would be honoured to run out onto. The barriers are there for one and all, the goal is clearly defined. Success starts with a label: front and rear L-plates that scream, in fluorescent hazmat yellow, STAY AWAY FROM ME. I'M A LEARNER!

Such is our reward; but what about the gruelling process that leads up to the stage of being able to sit for that precious piece of plastic which lets you control a car, legally, on the road? Once you have reached the magically assigned age of 16 you can sit for your "learners". Wait a minute: before you rush off to the AA you first have to study. No, no, not like for exams. Remember, you actually want your licence! What you can do is read a tedious book called *The Official New Zealand Road Code*. See, it is very official and makes reading an assigned English text look like a blast! Or you could take the path of least resistance and do quizzes online. Way more fun, and much easier. There are about 293 informative questions that cover everything to do with the car and road requirements. Found here: *www.drivingtests.co.nz* and here *www.aa.co.nz/drivers/roadcode-quiz*.

The actual test covers only 35 of them, with an optimistic 30-minute time limit. These questions are true, false or multi choice. Simple, you say. What are the optimum pass criteria, though? You can get up to three wrong and pass; any more than that, and you fail miserably. This means you have to sit again and pay another $93. Ouch! So passing first time is something you and your wallet want to do. Only after this milestone are you allowed to get into a car to learn to drive. *Honk, honk!*

Congratulations, you passed your learners! Those quizzes work wonders! You are now the proud holder of a New Zealand driver's licence with a typical photographic snapshot which if used on your passport would brand you as a terrorist or sinister criminal. Now it is time to start thinking about the next stage, your "restricted". There is an extended six-month delay before you can attempt this. You may look horrified but I'm sure your mother has told you about the benefits of delayed gratification. Who decides these time frames? Maybe it is a panel of scheming mothers who set these finicky incremental slots! For this stage, I personally recommend you take about three lessons with a professional driving instructor. They will teach you how to parallel park and do three-point turns. Things your devoted mother can never do. You can also sign up at *www.practice.co.nz*. This will give you a complete checklist of all the driving skills you will need to cover for your restricted test. Make sure you tick them once then tick them a second time as you practise and perfect each manoeuvre! Each new skill acquired is another step towards driving away.

Fast forward: six months have passed. I seriously hope you didn't crash into anything while learning! If you are feeling blissfully confident, book for your restricted and go for it!

Great! You're back, but you look a bit pale. Come, have a seat. I'll make you a cuppa while you tell me all about it. … The assessor failed you on a mere technicality? I'm sure: there's an extensive list of them. There is one assessor who will fail you before you even slide into the vehicle. The ladies are the more personable option. As you progress through life you will learn there will always be people who try to hinder. Just remember, you are down but not out, so move along.

If it helps to numb the pain it seems as though they, the Anonymous Authorities, have to fail about 60% of the people who attempt their licence. Now that makes me think, what car did you drive? A freaking four wheel drive! Are you crazy?!? Those cars are tanks! They have been dubbed "kid killers" for a reason. No wonder you failed! You should have driven a manoeuvrable Mini, a sleek Suzuki or a handy Honda Jazz, never a four-wheel drive or a muscle car. Oh, right, your frugal parents couldn't see the point of buying a car just for you? They already had two cars—a van and a four wheel drive—so you drove the smaller one! The gigantic nature of your car probably made failing easier! Maybe you should sit for your truck licence instead of your restricted or cosy up to some elderly folk in the New World car park and borrow their compact, fuel-efficient Chariot. Have you ever considered getting a real job and starting to finance your own fuel bill and activities? Yet another marker on the road of life. Oh well, give it another month and then re-sit.

Have you booked your test again? *Ka-ching!* Another $84.00, slight discount, really need that job. Thursday morning, 10:15 is a good time. The kids have been dropped off at school and most people are toiling away at work, so the asphalt paths to your success are quiet. The sun is respectfully positioned where it won't shine into your eyes and the driving assessors have just had their calming cup of caffeine. I warn you: be gracious, look behind more than you look at the road in front, don't forget railroad crossings. And finally, don't try to chat with the assessor, and whatever you do, avoid eye contact at all times! In life you sometimes have to orchestrate the advantages, look for them, plan for it, be ready to run the gap and hey presto. …

You passed! Do you feel elated? I did. You had a female assessor this time, who engaged with you as a person. Unbelievable! I bet that, as soon as you heard that you passed, you victoriously stripped the L-plates from your car faster than your parents were ever able to take the trainer wheels off your first bicycle. I gather your parents were blown away by your win and … only a *little* afraid for the future! The assessor who flunked you last time, had taken three students for their test while you were out. Three in your rapid 45 minutes! They would have all bombed. Poor them, dashed hopes, lost dreams, money down the drain. Sob! Not for you though. You can zero your trip-meter now you've got the green light!

Now you can go around shocking people who never took the time to observe you were out of dippers, and were the one behind the wheel! Ignite into action those teenaged boys who were mortified a girl beat them at their own game.

My final caution to you is that while you are on the road be extremely careful because only we, the younger generation, have been assessed so thoroughly that we actually know the road rules including recent changes, and therefore we drive safely. You should be the one driving the family around, as you are the most qualified. The screaming will diminish over time as they become more relaxed. You know you have made it when your mother continues to text as you approach a roundabout!

The "simple" act of attaining your learners, then your restricted, and the cumulative events along the way serve to illustrate you have arrived at a new stage. Congratulations, you have passed into glorious freedom. *Vroom, vroom!*

BRIDGET WHITE

Invigilation

Anxiety circles its prey
spindly legs drawing it closer and closer
ghosting over the intricate trap.

A suffocating silence
descends on the room.

The prey shudders with dread
glances around fidgeting.
No one can save it
it's already ensnared.

Tick tick tick

Pincers snap, pens click
time drawing closer
sweaty layer building
heart rhythm increasing.

Tick tick tick

The web of unease trembles.
Predator on the move.

ZOË LEVACK

Factory Girl

I'm a factory girl in a factory world
my hair is factory straightened
and factory curled.

My friends come in factory boxes
and stand in factory rows.
We play with factory toys
and wear factory clothes.

You glare when I start up
my factory phone
and you tut when I sit
on my factory own.

You sneer at my face
and sigh at my words.
You think that factory girls
should be seen and not heard.

On the other side of town
live the factory boys
with their factory sports
and their factory noise.

Some girls like them
and give them factory kisses
but others respond to their catcalls
with hisses.

The machines pump out the boys
building one by one.
There's a boy with a book
there's two more with a gun.

But I'm a factory girl.
I hold a factory knife
because the factory boys
think that they own my life.

Nobody likes the factory girls
with their factory ruffles and their factory curls.
We all are different in our hand-made clothes
we all are separate in our factory rows.

But people don't see that.
They think we're to blame
but wasn't it you
who made the factories, again?

CAROLINE SHEPHERD

Girls

and girls are so endlessly interesting
they lend hair ties and spot the extra dollar bus fare
tell you about smudged mascara and
cover you with their pastel umbrellas.

my friends tangle themselves
together
at lunch, their laughs
spill over the table and drip onto the floor
as we throw chips and talk until our voices
just fall out of our throats and onto our math books.

LEAH DODD

Blue Lightning

That Tuesday night you were blue lips in slow cars
you chewed milk duds and worried about the thunder
while my teeth were caramel and my hair came down
and it all felt soft like the middle of being a teenager
intentionally unsure and grinning anyway
like spilling hot coffee and driving too fast
or thumbing through memories like pages
and feeling waves spit onto our cheeks
each night better than the next; each kiss
like lightning; blue and ready for the thunder

PETRA WILLIAMSON

Trust Her to Spill

She is an arbitrary constant to me …
she exists. Has been present in my life.
Hell, she was even important to it
at one time.
Still, I question her value.

Don't get me wrong,
she isn't worthless.
Even mosquito larvae
have a purpose in life,
despite being at the bottom
of the food chain.
But to me?
She adds nothing.

When she told me she was leaving –
hollow aching.
But through the months to her coming
departure …

the enemy,
replaced the friend.

Tell me why I should hang on
to someone who spills
everything
before she leaves.

I wanted her to leave
so I could start to miss her.
I wanted her to leave
before I started to hate her.
I wanted her to leave
before she became nothing to me.

She didn't leave soon enough.

ERIN HUTCHINSON

Memories

Remember the day
we laughed as
a moon crested
the hill
your smile shimmered
in the glow
and my hair caught fire
in the early evening light.

Remember the day we walked
down the beach
next to waves of thunder
the wind picking up
glitter-like sand
to throw in our faces
drops rained down
smearing the ground
and we laughed
held onto each other
and walked on.

Remember the night I dared you to yell
pineapple
at the boys
when we were camping
we were snuggled together in our own little sanctuary
and we laughed when Lachlan's
face peered into our tent
and we three
talked into the day.

I remember the day I shied
away from your green
gaze
the day I lost faith
in those never ending days
perhaps you saw a glimmer of the future in your sleep
and all the jokes
of cat ladies got to you
but that day I saw
a rift grow
as you drew back
and I broke.

REBECCA KINGSWELL

Maladroit Mechanisms

Inside my mind is an
intricate piece of
machinery that is always moving,
whirring, clicking,
thinking.

Sometimes it whirs and clicks
too slow.
WHIR... CLICK... WHIR... CLICK.
Other times it goes too fast.
WHIRCLICKWHIRCLICK
and my focus darts
from one thing
        to
the
              next,
unable to handle the numbing pressure
that has begun to make the machine
inside my head rattle with uncertainty.

Always ticking over things *twice*, panicking at *pauses*,
"Did I say something wrong?"
It *never* stops, *never* slows.
WHIRCLICKWHIRCLICK.
A hundred thousand hammers
pound at the strong machine walls, attempting to fix
what was *never* broken.

Words that were *never* said
return to me as a tormenting
echo and the gears begin to
malfunction.
WHIRCLUNKWHIRCLUNK.
The hammers hit harder with the strongest punches
but to no avail.
WHIRCLUNKSNAPWHIRCLUNKSNAP.
And then the war begins: "Hello."

WHIRCLICK.
Collect the information,
recall the past and
form the strongest reply.

"Hi."
The heart-shaped cog speeds up,
beating bashfully with
every
passing
silent
second.
BOOMBOOMFLUTTERBOOMBOOMFLUTTER.
Nothing.

Did my carefully planned response
fall apart like the mechanism in my mind?
BOOMBOOMFLUTTER.
WHIRCLUNKCLANK.
An explosion of delicate
damaged gears
murders my thoughts without an
inkling of mercy, after a
grenade of doubt
strikes home.
"How are you?"
WHIRCLICKWHIRCLICK.
And it begins again.

SAMANTHA JORY-SMART

A Sketch of my Mind

I pluck the pulses
from my temples
        they aren't the stones I thought they'd be

wings flutter in my palms
membranes thrum with thought

tattooed upon their gossamer skins
my wrists sticky-thread veins
are an intricate design of a temple

thoughts pervade the rooms,
ideas form claret corridors,
memories—a far off, murky sea

wisps of lyrical words twist
into ropes of poetry

Slightly Nebulous and Mildly Insane

Victoria!!!!!

Talofa! It's me, Amelia, coming to you from way up here in the tropical north! All right, I'll admit, Auckland's not exactly the tropics, but hey, it's pretty close, right? So how's life in the capital so far? Breezy, I'm sure. I just moved into my hall last weekend, and I am SO EXCITED. For instance, let me describe my arrival for you:

> *[It is early morning, late in February; and the first tendrils of crisp autumn have begun to creep into the air. Somewhere in the distance an orchestra can be heard, beginning the familiar majestic melody of Holst's* Jupiter. *The camera pans the street, coming to rest on a young woman lugging three suitcases, a goldfish and a pot-plant called Steve. Naturally, she is managing the exorbitant quantities of luggage with astonishing grace and finesse. As the orchestra swells to the peak of its crescendo, she steps into a conveniently positioned shaft of sunlight, right in the centre of the street. All around, passers-by pause and turn to look. One by one, she sets down her bags; then, chin raised, she flings her arms out wide. And after a suitably dramatic pause…]*
> *Amelia: Why hello there, World. My name is Amelia, and I have arrived.*
> *All around, people begin to cheer. Trumpets sound, dolphins turn somersaults, and cupcakes fall from the sky. For in that moment they all knew: something extraordinary was about to begin.*

Okay, so maybe cupcakes didn't fall from the sky, but the rest happened practically word for word, I swear. I just feel this glorious sense of somethingness, you know? Can't wait for class tomorrow. Literature, here I come!

Hope all is dandy with you too,

Amelia

Amelia,

Hi! I'm glad to hear that you're enjoying Uni life so far. We've had a week of class now, and it's all really interesting. I feel as though I've learnt more chemistry in the past week than we did in a whole term at school, which is somewhere between cool and daunting. It's funny, though, the people aren't at all like I'd expected. I mean, at school there were all sorts—people who wanted to be interested in science but struggled even with algebra, people who probably could have been great but couldn't care less about anything to do with grades, people who could simultaneously make you feel like the most stupid person in the room and yet are embarrassed for doing well, all at the same time. I guess I'd always thought Uni would be different, that everyone in my classes would care about Chem like I do. But it's not like that at all, it's just school all over again, which is … well I guess it's okay. I mean, we had fun at school. Didn't we?

Aside from that, Wellington seems lovely so far. All the buildings are so tall, and the roads are so full of people all the time, which is kind of exciting. (I haven't seen any cupcakes falling from the sky though. We must be too far south for that!)

Anyway, I have to write out some redox notes, so I'll say good bye for now. Hope your first week of class went well,
Victoria

Vicky,

Well so far, I think the sagacious Mr Dickens hit the nail on the head when it comes to First Year: *It was the best of times, it was the worst of times. It was the age of wisdom, it was the age of foolishness.* Not that he was actually describing student life, but still, it seems pretty shrewd to me. For instance, this is what I overheard when we were walking home from town the other night:

> *[Three young men sit on the Symonds Street footpath. One is moderately tall, with gelled hair in the so-generically-good-looking-it's-completely-forgettable kind of way; one is smartly dressed but suspiciously red-faced; and the third is wearing shorts, knee-length khaki socks and a poncho that might once have been a tablecloth. Definitely a Fine Arts student. They are talking philosophically, or at least, they appear to think so.]*
> *Hair Gel: Wow. I mean, like, aren't stars, like, amazing, ya know?*
> *Poncho (nodding sagely): It's like the universe has turned on the lights so we can find our way home.*
> *Hair Gel: Did ya know that, like, every single element in the WORLD except hydrogen and helium was formed in the middle of a star, like, squillions of years ago. Ya know?*
> *Red Face: WOAH. Guys, guys, look at the MOON. It's GLOWING.*
> *Hair Gel (aside): Shut up Gary. (To Poncho): Maaate, you should come to my Gen-Ed. It's, like, Astro 101, yeah?*
> *Poncho (still nodding): Cool, bro.*
> *Red Face: GUYS! We should put a road cone on the MOON!*
> *Poncho: Liam, bro, don't you have a MedSci test tomorrow?*
> *Hair Gel. Crap.*

Oh to be young and to have imbibed just enough alcohol to appreciate the sentiments of the drunk.
Gloriously youthful,
Amelia
P.S. Don't you worry, Vicky, I would NEVER drink the night before a test. You've trained me well, I promise.

Amelia,

Your Poncho/Hair Gel friends sound like the people on the floor above me. Half the time I'm not sure whether they've even bothered to enrol. Maybe I should be spontaneous, just get a bottle of something and go up and join them ... but no, I never had your talent for mingling. Besides, I wouldn't know the first thing about buying wine. (Do students even drink wine??) Oh well. I guess more study time is a good thing, right?
Hope you're well,
Victoria

Vicks,

I am indeed well. Quite well, in fact, because there is a debonair young gentleman who has just joined my Interpreting Folktales paper, going by the name of Jack. We're several weeks into the semester, and no one knows where he's been all this time. It's all very mysterious. Mr Conan Doyle would have a field day, I'm sure.

Anyway, darling, how is all the chemistry going. Blown anything up lately? Oooh, ooh, do you get to wear lab coats in class? As the Pink Ladies said to Sandy, tell me more! Much love,
Amelia
P.S. Trust me Vicky, alcohol isn't nearly as fun as it's cracked up to be. It makes people slower than the heartbeat of a Blue Whale; which for you, with your beautiful brain, would be nothing short of a tragedy. But hey, seriously, is everything okay? Do you want to chat? I'm right here if you need me ☺

Amelia,

It was so lovely of you to call the other night. Please don't worry about me too much, though. I know I sounded stressed on the phone, but it was just because I had a test coming up, that's all. But yes, I promise I will take more study breaks from now on, as per your request. I might go to Te Papa for an afternoon. That could be fun. And as for the chemistry, well, I like it, I do, but I just can't picture myself working as a chemist once I graduate. Is that normal, so early on in my degree? Maybe it is. I'm probably worrying over nothing.
Hope all is well up there in Auckland,
Victoria
P.S. And no, Amelia, we don't wear lab coats to lectures ☺

Vicky,

All right then, I'll try not to worry too much about you. But Vicks, swear you'll talk to somebody next time you're feeling stressed or lonely or, I don't know, having a chemical crisis of faith, even if it's not me, yeah? You haven't said much about the people on your floor, but I'm sure you've met some lovely folk who'd be more than happy to lend an ear. And about the chemistry, it is SUPERLATIVELY okay to be uncertain about where it's going to take you. As long as you're enjoying the content, not every bit of learning has to have a purpose. You've got *years* to figure that bit out. And even if Chem doesn't seem that great right now, give it a chance, because after all Victoria, this is you. This is the girl who sang "the Elements" for our Year 8 talent quest. This is the girl who announced, at age 15, that she was going to be New Zealand's next Ernest Rutherford. If you love it that much, even if there aren't any careers waiting right now, somehow I've got the feeling that you'll forge a whole new type of career, one that's exactly like you always wanted, because I know you, Vicky. That's just the kind of thing you'd do.
Your number one fan,
Amelia,
P.S. Jack and I had a picnic in the domain yesterday! He really is quite the gentleman. If you were here, we would have to take a turn about the room together, à la Elizabeth Bennett, so that I could tell you all about it.

Amelia,

Thank you; really, it's very sweet of you to care so much, but don't you worry about me. I'll be, as you'd say, just dandy, I'm sure. Everything's going much better this week, though. I don't have any tests for another week or so, and I've even been invited to go out for afternoon tea with some of the girls from my floor; so that was thoughtful of them. And ooh, exciting about the mysterious Jack! I hope the picnics continue!
Victoria

Victoria,

Calamity has struck! Much like lightning in fact, but less likely to cause a power cut. Allow me to explain:

> *AMELIA: the Stage Production Based on a True Story, Act III, Scene iv.*
> *[Amelia enters stage left, wearing a shirt which declares* EXIT, *pursued by a bear. She appears slightly nebulous and mildly insane. The audience smiles in recognition of the character they have come to know and love. Or at least know. Amelia (as she has done for the last several weeks) glances across the tutorial room to the far desk, where a certain handsome young man sits, with an empty seat by his side. Smiles (i.e.   ) and heads for the empty seat.]*
> *** 27 hours later ****
> *[Amelia returns to stage, wearing a (mildly soggy)blue top and a Deathly Hallows necklace, speaking to herself in vaguely Shakespearian prose. The scene looks much the same, bar the writing on the whiteboard, which now reads* The Brothers Grimm: *did they seriously think those were children's stories?*
> *Amelia walks toward her usual desk. She senses something is wrong, and frowns (i.e. ☹). Suddenly realising the problem, she draws back in horror; or, to quote Oscar Wilde, sways like a plant with fingers outstretched: the incessantly punctual Jack is nowhere to be seen.*
> *The audience gasps, shocked at the sudden turn of events. There is an outbreak of muttering to the tune of* Qu'est-ce que c'est?, *"Didn't we pay to see a crappy but happy, generic American storyline?', "You're standing on my toes", etc.*
> *A crescendo of suspenseful orchestral music is heard as the curtain comes down for half-time. Members of the audience stand up and meander out to purchase expensive ice creams and small glasses of juice. They are left pondering why the playwright had such an obscure change of direction at this stage in the play (Did he have a heart attack? Did he lose his plot notes?) and wait in suspense for the second half to begin.]*

He's just... gone. Poof! Vanished without a trace, like the mysterious Amy Dunne. Arrrgh, it's driving me crazy, Vicky. What if he's left for good? How is a girl supposed to write an essay on Orwell when all she wants to do is stick her head out the window and yell loudly at fate, until the people from 4th floor tell her to shut up and go to bed?
Suitably anguished,
Amelia

To the wonderful Victoria,
Please excuse my impatience at writing again before you had the chance to reply, but...

[Amelia reappears on stage, amid rainbows and cupcakes and fairy bread.(A small marching band descends from the ceiling— a drum and a few trumpets would be appropriate. Or, if these cannot be sourced, a recorder would do.]
Amelia: (singing at the top of her lungs, waking the goldfish from his afternoon slumber) Yipidee doo dah, Yipidee day; my, oh my, what a wonderful day! Plenty of sunshine, plenty of rain (I think I might have these lyrics wrong; they don't quite seem to make sense) Yipidee doo dah, Yip - ah - dee - daaaaaaaaaaaaaaaay!
[And if the audience can't follow the above amendment to the script, here is a clue: Guess who's just re-appeared in tutorials?]

The dashing Jack has returned! Aah, Vicky dear, he is simply glorious. He has all the chiselled cheekbones of Mr Rochester, but none of the there's-a-mad-woman-in-my-attic shadows under his eyes. Of course, my desire to be his Jane does not extend quite so far as to be willing to go blind for him like she did, but I'm sure I can find a happy compromise. You know, keeping my eyes shut while I'm asleep or something. And what about you, Vicks? Any prospective husbands on the horizon?
Love always,
Amelia

Amelia,
Well I don't know about husbands but, um, there is this boy that I sit next to at dinner sometimes. Oliver. He's quiet too, but not in a shy way, if that makes any sense. We sort of went out for coffee on Tuesday, and I think he's going to ask me out again. Well, maybe. We'll see. Anyway, sorry, I'm probably boring you terribly, so I'll stop being gushy.
Hope your essay writing went well.
Victoria

Vicky,
"Stop being gushy"?!? Victoria, my dear girl, if that's what you're calling gushy then I can see we've got a long way to go. Details, Vicky darling! What floor is he from? What does he study? Is he unflinchingly supportive of your dreams to be the next Marie Curie? If not, you send him straight up to Auckland, and I'll give him a proper talking to.
Promise you'll tell me about him, though, won't you: where he's from, how he smiles, what he thinks of classic literature. You know, all the important things.
Oh, and his surname, please, so that I may undertake the obligatory Facebook stalk. Ears wide open,
Amelia

Amelia,
Well, he's tall. I mean, he's taller than me; though I guess that's not saying much. He's doing a BA like you—Ancient History though, not Comparative Literature. But I'm sure he is suitably appreciative of the written word, as per your instructions. He's from my hall, 3rd floor—hence the eating dinner together—although he's half Italian on his mother's side, so he's always announcing that the hall food is *disgustoso* compared to what he cooks at home. Oh, but he's ever so sweet, Amelia. Yesterday I was sitting out on the floor 7

balcony to absorb some Vitamin D, and he called me, completely out of the blue, just to ask if I was having a nice day. It's silly, I know, but it really does feel lovely just to know that someone is thinking of me.

Sorry if I'm boring you,

Victoria

P.S. And his surname is Miscota, by the way.

Oliver Miscota? OLIVER MISCOTA?!? Don't you know who he is, Vicky?

Aaarggh, so excited for you!!!

Practically giddy,

Amelia

Um, no? Who is he?

Victoria

Oh, all right then, since you asked. HE'S YOUR ROMEO!!!!

Let me explain.

1. He's Italian.
2. You're from feuding families. (I mean, arts kids and science kids are always talking smack to each other, aren't they?)
3. He called up to you on your balcony, as per the classic wherefore-art-thou moment. And for the grand finale…
4. I'm approximately one hundred and thirteen per cent sure that his name is an anagram.

Here, I'll show you:

You just take the letters from Oliver Miscota, switch them up a bit, and voila: VIC'S ROMEO TAIL. Hmm. Okay, what about… O MISTICAL ROVE. Not quite. Ooh, ooh, wait, I've got it:

* cue drumroll *

… VICTORIA'S ELMO!!!

See? I told you. Okay, fine, fine, it's not what I promised, but honestly, Elmo, Romeo; Potayto, Potahto. It's basically the same thing. I'm telling you, Vicky, it's practically Destiny. Feel free to text me the wedding dates any time, Mrs Miscota.

Love always,

Amelia

Oh Amelia,

Sometimes you're worth your weight in gold. I can't promise anything in the way of wedding invites, but I will keep you updated. And hey, we'll see each other in the holidays (can you believe it's been four months since I last saw you?) so maybe you can meet him then. He's such a sweetheart, though; he always seems to know when I'm stressed, and he always calls to calm me down, even if he's got plenty of his own assignments to stress about at the time. Anyway, exams start in a week, so I'm off to study.

Victoria

Vicky,

Off to study? I don't buy it for a second. Off to the harbour-side, no doubt, for a romantic sunset stroll. Skipping study to hang around with eligible bachelors? How scandalous! Then again, Shakespeare did say, "Love is merely a madness". And Shakespeare has a funny way of being right about most things.

Anyway, I'm terribly sorry to cut this short, but I too have exams to study for. And yes, I DO mean actual study, none of these sunset stroll fandangles. Although, Jack and I have been going on rather a lot of those lately. ...

Suspensefully,

Amelia

P.S. Good luck for your exams. I'm sure you'll do brilliantly, you clever cookie, you.

Amelia,

Sounds like somebody's having fun up there in Auckland! Anyway, sorry, I really can't talk because I've got two exams tomorrow, so I just wanted to say: hope you're well, good luck to you too, and yes, I AM doing actual study. Mostly ☺

Victoria

P.S. Looking forward to seeing you so we can chat properly. Only a fortnight to go!

Victoria,

Well this week has been as monotonous as the grounds of Thornfield when Jane visits for the first time: exams, study, more exams, more study, you know the drill. I don't think I've ever studied so much in my life. Revision doesn't agree with the soul, my dear, don't you find? Of course you don't. Oh, and, uh, this happened:

> *[It's Friday night and the last exam wrapped up hours ago. There is a general atmosphere of euphoric exhaustion in the hall, and throughout the corridors students can be heard making celebration plans: "Let's go to Bar 101", "let's go to a movie", "let's join a knitting club" sort of thing. Jack and Amelia are sitting in the common room, chatting.]*
>
> *Amelia: Do you want to go see a film?*
>
> *Jack: Actually, I–*
>
> *Amelia: Or we could join a knitting club if you want?*
>
> *Jack (with a sudden burst of unwanted honesty): Amelia, I don't think we should see each other any more.*
>
> *Amelia (profoundly):*
>
> *Jack: I, uh, have to go now. Err, goodbye? (silence falls as he exits, stage left)*
>
> *Amelia (turns to the audience and shrugs): I guess he's not a fan of knitting, huh? (Then suddenly, her composure crumbles and, centre-stage, she falls to her knees, tears streaming silently down her face. As if sensing her despair, all puppies in the vicinity cease wagging their tails, and the moon vanishes behind several layers of ashen cloud. In the background, a mournful rendition of "Somebody That I Used To Know" begins to play. Shrouded in gloom, the scene ends.)*

IT'S ALRIGHT VICKY, I'M KIDDING!!! I mean, he did break up with me, but it wasn't anywhere near that dramatic. And oh well, right? Same old story: plenty more fish in the sea, plenty more Darcys in the ballroom.

Anyway I, uh, have to go, so goodbye.

Amelia

Don't you go thinking you can pass this off as nothing serious, I KNOW you really liked him. Are you okay? Is there anything I can … actually, you know what, this is ridiculous. Stay right where you are. I'm going to call you.

Vicky darling!
Thank you for the lovely telephone call, and for the ice cream you sent me, even if it was mildly melted! But honestly, I'm just grand. Don't you fret about me. I can't believe our first semester (well, trimester for you) is already over. How time has flown. Just think, in five semesters from now, you'll be a chemist and I'll be a … actually, what will I be? People who study anthropology are anthropologists and people who study history are historians, but I've never heard a term for people who study comparative literature. Hmmm. I think from now on, I shall be known as a Comparatorial Literaturologist. We could set up a business together, Chemists & Literaturologists Consulting Inc. Sure, the clientele might be a bit weird, but as business names go, there's a definite ring to it.
Feeling qualified (and thoroughly ready for a holiday),
Amelia
P.S. SEE YOU TOMORROW!!!

PORTIA BAINE

Trying to Decide

on a university course structure
but this one fly keeps
getting
on my
nerves.
                    Circling around my head

then buzzing past my ear as if to tell me a secret.

I try to focus on how on earth I'm going to choose a degree
but then it lands on my arm

            maybe trying to offer advice?
            I remember when I was a maggot myself.…

I hit it with the prospectus.

A wing twitches.

I think

that's quite enough advice for one day.

MIA SUTHERLAND

Remembering Summer

Yellow heat,
bleeds from the sky
no one is playing
it's far too hot for that.

Against the light
green grass pales to feeble brown.

Feathers nestle in the silence
none brave enough for flight
it's far too hot for that.

Trees reach out
to offer shade

the bark
shrinks

it's not too hot to crack.

HAROLD COUTTS

Temperature Performance Piece

air on arm hairs playing discordant tunes
but the chill is centre stage
bowing under the lights, icicles far from dripping
as the curtain kisses the wood panels
a crowd cheers

a text tone in heat ends a slumber
lazy recognition is framed artwork
crooked on the wall but not so dusty
the gallery is quiet today

the lip of a curb is comfortably complacent in fever
seasoned with the dregs of footsteps
the waiter serves it fast

the press of you in sheets is potpourri
cold is close but I nestle the bowl

temperature is imprinted in my sculptured skin

PORTIA BAINE

An Egyptian Goddess—or Maybe Just a Cat

A Burmese interrupts café sleep to pad across the floor and jump onto her favourite table—the one in the corner next to the window where she can better watch the night. Flicking her tail, she reminds the occasional passer-by of her presence. Light from an adjacent streetlamp diffuses through the window just enough to illuminate the contours of her blue-grey coat. Statue-like, her colouring and posture parallels the basalt form of Bast. The goddess sits and waits, measuring time by the periodic flicking of her eyelids.

A man walks past the café window—a nightly routine—shoes scuffing the pavement, unenthusiastic walking for a destination many hours away. He smells of disappointment and cigarettes. His tan coat, dulled by age and poor street lighting, identifies him as homeless, but he is as much attached to it as he is to this ritualistic walk towards morning. Modern day nomadism demands that you keep both eyes rather than one open, and he achieves this through uninterrupted movement.

Yet the figure in the window stops him in his travels. She sits perfectly still save for the twitch of an ear to acknowledge his presence, and when he puts his face to the window the better to see her, she holds his gaze as humans do not. Unmoving, the golden eyes so prized in her breed regard the bloodshot brown of his. Seconds or hours pass where neither creature moves. Each watches the other—each watched by the other.

A faint police siren is heard in the distance. The cat begins to clean herself, and the man moves on.

MONIQUE THORP

Explorers

my friends have gone to
tangle
in neon-vined jungle
while I stay home and glow the window

beyond the waver of the glass
they pave a messy path
and come home mixed
and mangled

Sticky Streets

We're walking through melted
tarmac streets
and scuffing
the sidewalk grasses that peep
through yellow gravel
there's hot cement stuck to your shoes
the clammy hands
trying to hold onto your phone
time check
sweating underneath that nylon hoodie
and those highlighted bangs sticking to your face.

I don't know if we're laughing or crying
because it's raining
even as we see the heat
spiralling up through steamed windows
wet asphalt
with rain coursing down your eyelids
pooled.

Can we go now?
there's another street ahead and
it's one where the footpath
doesn't drag you down
but we've said that for the last few blocks
and the street signs keep breaking.

Catch Me if You Can

"Don't you think it's strange?"

"What?"

"Well, don't you ever wonder how many people you'll pass, in your lifetime, without as much as a glance, a hello, a good-bye?"

"No, I don't need to."

"I know, I know, but don't you think it's strange?"

"I couldn't possibly talk to everyone."

"But you might miss something, someone important–"

"Is it not enough?"

"What?"

"The people you meet. Having the experiences you've had, will have."

There's a pause as the young woman studies the young man who has spoken. His eyes are closed and the crescent moons beneath them are tinted indigo. He occupies most of the single bed in her small, rented flat.

"You mean you?" she says eventually.

"No, no. I just mean, why do we need to meet everybody? Hell, why would you want to? Besides, you'd never have enough time. You'd waste your whole life meeting people, and it's not possible, so why worry?"

"I'm just saying it's strange how many people go by without you ever really knowing they existed. You can live in the same town for years and years and never meet. But you can go to Paris on a whim and meet the love of your life. It's just odd, is all."

"Yeah, I guess."

Another pause.

"Oh god, sorry that was …."

"No, no, it's fine."

"It's the cider, I swear. Can't bloody shut my trap."

"'Course."

"Makes you sleepy, I think."

"Mmm."

"Irritable, maybe? Apathetic–"

The young man frowns, his sulky lips upturned.

"Oh my—*sorry*! God, I'll just shut up now."

"Hmm, 's alright."

"Really, I'm sorry."

"Yeah, it's okay. You're right, that cider does loosen your jaw—and your morals.

He smiles, full of self-satisfaction, and kisses her shoulder where her t-shirt has slipped, revealing an area of smooth olive skin.

"Huh. Well, if you're not careful, I'll soon loosen your pretty white teeth."

"Oh yeah?"

"Yes."

"I never took you for a fighter, Bea. I thought you had a … now how did you put it … *pacifist approach to life.*"

"I can give it up anytime, *Jas.*"

"That would figure."

"What do you mean by that?"

"Oh, nothing."

"No, say."

"Well, you lot seem to get your panties in a twist over the war or whatever, claiming it's only for the 'oil' and the–"

"It is!"

"In two years it'll probably all be over and forgotten."

"And what do you mean by 'you lot'?"

"Oh… never mind. Forget I said anything."

"No. Tell me what you meant."

"Oh, Bea!"

"Beatrice!"

"Fine. Beatrice. I just meant from where I'm standing it looks like your pacifist badge of honour is actually nothing other than a badge, and as soon as you leave here you'll forget you ever cared, and carry on your merry way."

"That's not true!"

"Well, that's how it comes across."

"I should've known. You're so …"

"What?"

"Ah, stuff it. What's the point of this?"

"What's the point? What's the *point*? We're lying in your bed, and we're arguing about pacifism and how it's such a pity that we can't meet everybody, that's the *bloody point*!"

"God, I knew it! I knew you were pissed about something."

"Well damn it, Beatrice, I didn't come here to confer! I swear it's all you do these days."

"Well maybe you should find someone who doesn't bore you, Jasper, with so much talk. Hey, here's an idea! Why don't you just buy a spa-bath, for god's sake, and be done with it? It's all wet and warm, eases your aching bones and only gets bubbly when you want it to!"

Whipping the bed covers off her body, she rolls out of the bed, naked except for a large, loose grey T-shirt. She picks her crumpled jeans off the cold wooden floor and furiously starts to yank them on.

"Ah, shit, Bea. It's not just that."

"Then what, huh?"

She freezes, jeans halfway up her thighs.

"It's just—jeez, you're like, so bloody uptight that you can't have any fun!"

"I can so have fun!"

"All right then. Show me."

"Excuse me?"

"Go on, prove it."

"I do not have to prove any–"

"See! All talk. No action."

"Yeah, getting some "action" is all you ever worried about!"

"So? At least I'm honest about it. And you know that's bullshit, I just get sick of talking about the same bloody things. You know, when did it ever hurt to stop worrying about everything so much and just talk about–"

"What?"

"I don't know! The weather, or something relatable or familiar, at least!"

"You want to talk about the weather. ..."

"You know what I mean. I just think you need to stop over-thinking all the time and have a little fun. Stop caring so much."

They stare at each other in silence. A moment passes. The girl sighs. She crosses her arms melodramatically.

"So?"

"So, get back into bed, you."

"Jasper, this is my flat. You can't tell me what to do."

"Tough luck. Get back into bed, Bea. Come on."

"It's Beatrice."

"Yeah, yeah, so you keep telling me."

She holds her ground for a few moments. But the wooden slats are cool on her bare feet, and the bed is enticing. She rolls off her jeans, leaving them abandoned and crumpled on the floor, and slides back in the warm bed to lie next to him.

"I don't know why I put up with you," she says. "You're insufferable."

"Insufferably sexy."

She groans. A smile splits across his face.

"You really are a pain in the arse."

"Bea?"

"Yeah?"

"There's only so much a man can take."

"Oh right, right. Sorry." *There's a brief pause as she contemplates her apology.* "But you are."

"Yeah, well, you're not perfect either, Bea ... Beatrice."

Another pause. They lie awkwardly in the cramped bed, shoulders overlapping. His back is propped up by a bunch of thin pillows. She is wedged under his armpit, her breath tickling his bare chest. For a time they both stare into nothingness: she at the ceiling and he at the curtained window.

"Don't you think it's strange we're together? You know, when there are so many other fish in the sea?" she says at last.

He exhales heavily through his nostrils. "Well, I didn't, but now come to think of it–"

She hits him in the arm playfully, but with just enough force to make it sting slightly.

"Hey! You're a big hypocrite if I ever met one," he exclaims.

"Yeah, well ... maybe if you didn't talk so much. ..."

They both start to giggle. Gently at first, then harder and more enthusiastically until their sides and cheeks ache.

"You, my sweet; my sweetest john dory of all gill-bearing aquatic craniate animals that lack limbs with digits ... are possibly the biggest catch of all. Now, settle down, will you? We've still got two hours before dawn and I don't want you wearing me out before I get to see the sunrise."

"Jasper!"

He laughs again and wraps both arms around her. He knows he's won. They both do.

NIKI MENZIES

La Belle Dame

A knight to love, and I to have
and hold; and a woman,
to keep, and a man to let her
go. Or maybe two, of one
this night, and soft lips caress
and bring new life to one
so cold, and yet to give
away her heart.

Come morning, fly,
from ill-fated dreams and find
a figure at the door
in glorious splendour, look upon his face,
and grace it with a maiden's smile.
A bed cannot hold a lover's warmth
whilst this new one shall stay a while.

Such time shall pass and slip away
as the shadow is forgotten,
and a new day dawns with strength
and words as soft as silk;
comfort comes as passion is sent from
this place, and I stay,
and the air I breathe is only his.

Fall victim to his honeyed words,
with the heaven's voice he doth proclaim
and claim to hold my heart
besides; but does she not shudder beneath
my gaze, as I for him,
in hidden ways?

Is it another touch I seek,
softer, a peach's furry cheek
that moves me—as his hands do not.
And yet, his velvet words
touch me in the name of another,
at God's own will he calls me his own.

And nights shall suffer,
split between a lover's lives,
caught up in two so different eyes

and one, with words shall hold my heart
as an angel might, but a soul sets apart
true desire I could never know.

A simple touch, and yet such a fiery trail
no words of his could so compare;
and there I see in her red blood
that flows through both our veins,
reclining in this moonlit place
her hair reflecting an internal
daze, which fades as we two
lovers sleep.

Awakened by a fleeing lark;
such forewarned sense only birds shall hold,
for flying with the angels changes
a feathered soul. Underneath a fallen yew
he comes to me,
the morning dew
hiding troubles on my cheek;
and he holds me, tells me what
he now doth know.

Red hair and blood, sleeping on in bliss;
and should I have touched her
one last kiss and raised her cheek's
furry down; a grace never to be bestowed
as I left her on the dewy ground,
a steadfast hand in mine, led away –
and as his, heaven's, words proclaimed,
loved a man 'til my last day.

NAIN ALFANTE

To Sir Peter Jackson

On *The Hobbit: The Battle of the Five Armies*

Place: Westfield Cinema (again)
Time: Just finished the midnight screening (see, because I was actually excited)
Mood: Like the butter of optimism scraped over too much bread

Do you remember me, good Sir? I wrote you a letter last year about the previous instalment of the Hobbit trilogy and wasn't expecting to write to you ever again. I had assumed it was all water under the bridge, a disappointment that we had all accepted and moved on from, and that you might have learned your lesson.

Ah, the sensation of engulfing disappointment. Did you hear that crashing sound? That would be the sound of my and every other person in the audience's hopes just hurtling down, deeper than the very depths of Moria.

As you may have deduced, I am not exactly jumping with joy and hailing this film with hosannas.

Let's establish that I have accepted the fact that the movie wouldn't coincide or at least attempt to parallelise the original book. I've accepted it. I've mourned the lost hopes and premeditated scenes I came up with, in case I was put in charge of it. I've (kind-of) moved on. As the author of a few spin-offs from other stories myself, I believed there was a way to salvage the carcass of *Desolation of Smaug* and make *The Battle of the Five Armies* spectacular. I don't usually notice flaws in the film until the credits are rolling, but I have become adept especially since I saw the second film.

You can consider this my review/rant/constructive criticism. Please take a seat, because there is much to be said.

What I liked least about the movie was that it lacked subtlety. Take Stephen Fry's Mayor of Laketown, for instance. He's unthinking, unlikeable, and one can practically see the halitosis on his breath every time he speaks. To see him simply leaving with the town's treasure and kicking off a person trying desperately to board his barge as Laketown is set ablaze by a dragon inferno was, by every movie-goer's standards, overkill on the LOOK-I-AM-A-BAD-LEADER-WHO-WON'T-BE-MISSED button.

Subtlety—our digital generation knows every cinematic trick in the book, okay? It's rated PG-13. We're not five. We know if someone's bad, you don't need to keep repeating it.

Another example is the romantic subplot (subplot's a euphemism by the way) between Kili the dwarf and Tauriel the trophy redhead fighter she-Elf. That badly written love story that has a timescale of about a week and a half. You know what I'm talking about. It felt like this: Kili and Tauriel have a little moment, but Legolas interrupts. Kili and Tauriel part ways sadly as Legolas watches from behind. Kili and Tauriel are thinking about each other and then Legolas says his heart belongs to Tauriel. Did I mention there was a love triangle here? Because there is a love triangle. Have you noticed the love triangle yet? We

122

have one, you know. A love triangle, I mean. See? There are two guys in love with Tauriel. Audience, did you get that yet? We have a LOVE TRIANGLE.

Subtlety. Sometimes you miss it. Moreover, someone needs to shine a glaring spotlight on the utter cheesiness of the romantic lines. [EXCERPT: "Is this love? Why does it hurt so much?" the doe-eyed damsel asks as she mourns the dwarf she met about a week ago. The Elf King, forgetting her previous insubordination for the sake of the now-dead dwarf, answers: "Because it was real."] (Insert gagging here.)

There were many plot-holes and just generally weird events in the film as well; many questions left irritatingly unanswered. Why did Azog float under the ice when he was wearing iron armour? Where on earth did those mountain goats come from? What happened to the Arkenstone after the battle? Who cleaned up the mess after the war? What exactly was the Elven King Thranduil doing at Dale and why on earth did he bring the Laketown citizens food if he had nothing to do with them? Was Tauriel's "banishment" lifted after the battle or not? Why did the dragon Smaug's death occur before the title even came on screen? Why was the second movie cut short just to bring about a climax that takes place in the first few minutes of the next film?

The point here Sir, is that the final instalment of any series is not supposed to have unanswered questions. You cannot possibly get to the last movie and let events happen *deus ex machina* in order to get the plot moving. This film was riddled with shaky plot devices and character mutilations so that unsurprising deaths could be seen as redemption.

Speaking of shaky plot devices, I have to bring up the character of Tauriel again, and the misconstrued assumption in the majority of blockbuster films about the inclusion of female characters. You are not the only culprit I bare my fangs at for this, Sir—but I had hoped you would be an exception to this sickness in mass media instead of an example. Strong female characters are female characters who are well written, not just a female who knows how to carry a sword or bow. Strong female characters are not there to look good, throw a punch here and there, then spend the rest of the film doing absolutely nothing while the men continue to get things done. QED: Tauriel is not a strong female character but the thin shell of one.

Let me explain my indignation at this female character that, as stated by you in previous interviews, was meant to be the empowering female presence in an otherwise male-dominated film. Tauriel was intended to be a role model for girls, but I hardly want to accept a character whose intentions seem to only come from the male characters she is around. This unnaturally perfect female can let waist-long hair down while fighting, and barely acknowledges the other few female characters there. Did she look twice at Bard's daughters when their father was away trying to shoot down a dragon? What was a nimble Elven warrior doing on a boat in the middle of a dragon's attack when she could have rescued other civilians easily? With all due respect, Tauriel was the crowning disappointment of the trilogy—and this is a sentiment shared by the very group you were hoping to pander to. We're past having obligatory "tough" female characters that simply revert to the clichés we've been fighting against in the first place.

Perhaps I am overly critical based on my own standards for likeable characters and perhaps other people would have enjoyed the unrealistic fight sequences and cringe-worthy romances. Consequently, I shall now proceed to tell you what I was able to enjoy from the film. (This will be a short paragraph, no matter how hard I try.) Naturally, there were many positive aspects of the film which cannot be overlooked. Visually, the film was stunning. Establishing shots showing beautifully CGI-ed landscapes and amazing Weta Workshop costumes ticked off a few peeves simply because they took my breath away. The soundtrack was splendid as well, as I had every reason to assume. The orchestral pieces were able to tug at my heartstrings and give me shivers of anticipation where the dialogue fell short. Yes, the film was good there, and I commend you for that. What resulted in an ending that I was quick to leave after, was the storyline and its character development.

It's a shame, really. I would not dare, without due reason, to make such a negative report to the person who put New Zealand on the map for the film-making industry—hence it is so infuriating that I actually have due reason to complain; I don't want to! I wanted to enjoy the film like the other 150 people filling up the cinema on that midnight screening, not list its numerous sins.

Yet here we are, at the last of Middle Earth films, walking away with stooped shoulders instead of excited chatter. Well I am, at least. Perhaps people were right in saying the Lord of the Rings films ruined the film industry. You can't go any higher than perfection after all.

So if it's any consolation to you, while the Hobbit trilogy sputtered and died, the Lord of the Rings will continue to blaze throughout history. It's those films the rest of the world will remember you for.

But the Hobbit trilogy? Most likely from letters like this.

Ever a Lord of the Rings fan, I remain,

Rosie Cotton

HAROLD COUTTS

Fitness

my body aches with
the curve of a hip
tectonic plates shedding
familiarity
for new ground

the laugh of my growth
reverberates clear
my body is an endless
talk
looking for new content

LAURA HETHERINGTON

Nest and Frank

Nest didn't like birds. When people discovered her name they would say, "You must really love birds!" However, Nest despised them, and the fact that her name was literally the definition of a bird's house didn't help. "No, my parents like them, though, so I guess that sparked the idea for my name," was her rehearsed response for all the bird comments and questions. The fact was, everything about the arrow-tip beaked, dinosaur-feet creatures frightened her—animals that seemed to love the thrill of a car screaming towards them on the road, or the unconcerned ones with the nerve to snoop around your feet, looking for crumbs outside a café. No, Nest really didn't like birds. So when her parents (she called them the two hawks) presented her with a bright yellow canary for her fourteenth birthday, she was stunned into silence.

"Happy birthday," they shouted as they lifted the white sheet off a metal cage which Nest thought looked like a miniature jail. She stared, her mouth the shape of a perfectly oval egg. "Isn't he cute? He's only a couple of weeks old." The canary stared up at Nest. Its tiny black eyes pierced her dark brown ones and made it impossible to look away, however much she wanted to.

"Well, do you like him?" the hawks probed, suddenly nervous that it had all been a terrible mistake.

Nest's parents were artists and had met through a shared passion for painting, sketching and photographing two-winged creatures. When Julie had become pregnant, the name Nest had seemed perfect for two bird-lovers. It was obvious that, from a young age, Nest didn't share their passion. Yet, fourteen years later, that didn't stop them from trying to get their daughter onto the same page.

A small chirping sound brought Nest back to one of the strangest moments she had experienced in life. She picked up the cage, smiled at her parents and shut herself in her bedroom. "I'm calling you Frank," she told her new pet. "You probably don't like this situation as much as I do, so let's pretend, for the sake of the hawks, that everything is okay."

By the time dinner was eaten, cake was devoured and friends had come and gone, Nest was managing just fine with Frank. She had given him some chocolate cake crumbs, taken a photo and sent it to her favourite aunt, and even been brave enough to hold him while her friends ooh-ed and aah-ed over her yellow companion.

A week passed. Frank wanted to fly, but of course that wasn't an option in a cage hanging from a hook outside his new owner's window. Nest would have liked to sleep in more on the weekend, but hadn't yet mastered the art of sleeping through the bird's chirps. Secretly, both individuals were enjoying the inescapable presence of one another.

On the unforeseen day that Frank went missing, Nest cried. Not the inconsolable sort of cry that left people red in the face and gasping for air, but a small, inconspicuous weep that was almost silent.

It all started one Saturday morning when Nest woke up. Frank hadn't woken her up, which was very odd. She pulled back her curtains, to find herself staring at the flowerless cherry tree. That is, she was not seeing the tree through the bars of Frank's metal cage. This was lying on the ground with the little door open. An empty shell of a home. Nest gasped and ran out to the kitchen, where the two hawks were, one making coffee, the other artistically flipping egg-free pancakes made of buckwheat.

"Mum, Dad, Frank isn't in his cage!"

Her parents stared at her, surprised by their daughter's sudden outburst.

"What do you mean, honey? Are you sure?" her mother asked.

"His cage is on the ground and the door's open. He's gone!" Nest had begun to make a soft sniffling sound.

All three went out to survey the situation, only to find that Nest was correct. Frank was gone, the only reminders of his existence the sad looking cage and the half-full bird food packet in Nest's room.

"It must have been the wind last night, sweetie," her father said, picking up the empty cage. "It was pretty rough." He bundled Nest into a bear hug and let her cry into his shoulder.

Life went on for the now birdless family. Nest missed waking up to Frank's daily chirps, even though she had complained about them before. Her parents offered to buy her another bird but Nest reminded them she didn't like birds; she only liked Frank. So instead, her mother sketched a picture of the missing pet, framed it and hung it next to Nest's window. A friendly yet sad reminder of the friend Nest never expected to have.

She hoped that Frank was happy, finally able to stretch his bright yellow wings and see the world from above. She could almost imagine him sitting in the cherry tree that had now blossomed: a splash of yellow amongst pink flowers and green leaves.

In fact, that tree was Frank's favourite. From its branches, he could see Nest open her curtains every morning and stare straight at the very place he had been perched. He hoped she could see him, alive and free. What Nest soon came to realise was that the yellow dot in the tree *was* Frank. She was sure of it. He was the first and probably last bird she would ever have, because Nest didn't like birds. But she loved Frank.

JACINTA van der LINDEN

Now They're Gone

Did grief ever truly go away? Her friends, people who claimed to know, said that it did; that at the very least, it got easier. But now, as the sun rose steadily over the playa, its fingertips brushing the ranch in front of her, she wasn't so certain. The sight before her was stunning, ethereal. A bloody red glow radiated upwards and outwards, translucent tendrils of light standing out starkly against the barren landscape. The sagebrush, the dust, the ranch house at her back, all were tinted crimson as if drowning in gore; a reminder of the precarious existence they eked out in this desolate place. Death stalked its canyons, prowled its summits. Even the places they had tamed to their will were not immune to its touch. She had learned this the hard way.

Once she would have been awestruck by the sight before her. She would have stood entranced as the desert was lit, on fire with her at its centre. Now she took no notice. Life's beauty had lost its hold on her the minute it happened.

The intensity of her emotion had shocked her. She had begged, screamed for one thing: the chance to go back. Back to winter, that time of chaotic, dysfunctional belonging. She would have been feeding the horses, exposing herself reluctantly to the bitter morning chill. Snow the night before would have coated the yard with a fine layer. It would have swirled in eddies and currents sending pinpricks down her spine as it landed on the back of her neck. She would have hugged herself for warmth.

The sun had been a dull glow on the horizon, the morning quiet and peaceful, muffled snorts the only sound as the horses nosed about in the snow-covered yard. She had closed her eyes to savour the moment, only to have it torn away from her by a painfully loud voice at her back. It had chattered on, oblivious despite her wince, despite the fact that the horses had bolted, their panic a wildfire flaring through the neural pathways that interconnected the herd. Codey had clung ingratiatingly to her shirt, innocence written all over his pudgy, irritating face. She had ignored him, but he hadn't noticed. Never did. He couldn't see that she hated him and his mother. He was the brother she had never wanted, Alex the mother she had never needed.

So why was she the first to lose control on the day it happened? Why had it hurt so badly, as if a knife had slid between her ribs and was slowly gutting her? Why had she felt an inexplicable sense of horror at the look on her father's face? He thought she didn't care, that she was glad it had happened. She knew why. She had never wanted a brother, never needed another mother.

On the day when it happened, she thought Codey and Alex were merely late. Then they received the call. She was there when the doctors came out of the room. The sterile smell permeating her nostrils made her think not only of sickness and death, but of how it was such a cold, unfeeling place in which to die. She had listened in disbelief as they told her and her father they were sorry but there was nothing they could do. The words refused to sink in. She felt numb, as if wrapped in a bubble that made it impossible to comprehend what had been said. Then, all of a sudden she understood, and wished she hadn't.

She had never wanted a brother, never needed another mother. So why did she feel as if her heart was breaking?

ERIN DONOHUE

Coins

Now that visits to Nana and Grandad's
are just visits to Nana's,
I carry home memories of him like
coins in my pocket.

I let them clang against each other.

I remember
how he used to steal my nose
even when I was old enough to know
it was still on my face.
How we used to hug
when I first arrived and
before I left
because once just wasn't enough.
How I phoned to thank him
for the flowers he sent
and he said
they are as pretty as you are.

Most days I am poor.
My memory of him is weak and tired
and almost always second-hand.

But on the days I have coins,
I let them rattle loudly, hoping it lets me find more.
Stuffed between the couch cushions.
Hidden under the bed.
Stashed in the old faded
pink pig
money box that used to
sit on my shelf.

MARY LOCKER

Marmalade Tears

Oranges. That is my first memory. I remember my mother holding me up amongst the leaves of an orange tree so that I could reach out with my chubby hands and tug a juicy, golden sun from its branch.

Heat. That is my second memory. Of a sweltering kitchen, a vat of sticky marmalade bubbling away on the stove, and my mother pressing a spoon into my hand so that I could use it to make pretty patterns in the swirling concoction.

Laughter. That is my third memory. Of my mother and I laughing until our stomachs hurt, eating warm marmalade sandwiches, and putting leftover orange peel in our mouths and making silly faces at each other.

Laughter. That is also my fourth memory. Of my father coming home and tickling me until I was gasping for air, and then his pretending to laugh as I tried to imitate him.

Panic. That is my fifth memory. Of my mirth evaporating into fear as I watched my mother doubled over, heaving with violent coughs, and the feeling of helplessness because there was nothing I could do.

Confusion. That is my sixth memory. Of trying to slip through the door of my mother's bedroom, and not understanding why she wouldn't speak to me, and pressing my cheek into the palm of her hand harder and harder until I thought I saw a wisp of a smile cross her face.

Tears. That is my seventh memory. Of clutching my father so hard that it would have taken an age to prise me off him, and he holding me just as tightly, and both of us trying to weep away the realisation that we would never see my mother again.

These are my memories, my marmalade tears.

DUNCAN MATCHETT

I Live Under Your Bed Now

Not out of choice
it was the only place left.

I would have happily made
residence in your freezer
but your father has locked
himself in there
his hairy belly squeezed
between the meat pies and slicker pads.

I considered living in a suitcase
but your mother has filled them all
with everything she owns
and put them by the front door.

I went out into the back yard
to seek safety in your tree house
but all I could find
was the tree's old stump.

I checked beneath the couch cushions
but a family of weevils
have claimed the potato chips.

I almost got comfortable
in your attic
but I couldn't bring myself
to shift the photo albums
of you when
you were happy.

So here I am
but don't be scared
I'll keep you safe
and pay the rent
of putting the blankets back over you
when you kick them off
during the night.

SAM POLES SMITH

My Big Little Brother

"Wait up!"

I hear a muffled, monotonous voice that could only be Oliver's. I vault over the last log, stumble on an overhanging root, but regain my balance to beat Oliver to the creek. This creek was Oliver's second home, like a cot to a child, somewhere he feels safe and calm, and it has been like this for the 19 years of his life. The only sounds are bird chirps and cicada clicks. I gaze across the creek towards the silver ferns that arch over the bank like a hunched-over old man about to fall into the water. The shadows are drowned by a miserable blanket of decaying leaves which create a green, swamp-like coating, but Oliver loves it here, and that is all that matters. He never fusses with aesthetics, never judges anyone or anything by its looks, and feels love equally for the ugly and the beautiful. He can always discern the inner beauty of a person or a place.

"I win," I announce, in a cocky, egocentric tone which would wind any other person up, but not Oliver.

"Good job, Brad," he says without any hint of sarcasm. But that doesn't surprise me. Oliver is never aroused to anger when we are here, at least never to my knowledge. When he does get mad, inexplicable rage emerges out of nowhere, clouting him like a brick wall of fury. Mum says that it is normal for people like him whose brains have never fully developed. Doctors say he has the mental ability of a two-year-old and will always be too simple for school. *Too special for society*, they say. But although Oliver is clueless and clumsy at times, he is bright in his own special way. "Please be careful, Oliver," I say firmly, as he approaches the edge of the creek. He has a very large, rounded body, which makes him seem even clumsier.

"Please be careful, Oliver," he echoes, but he isn't mocking me. *Echolalia* is what people like Oliver have, Mum tells me. He reiterates things that are spoken to him, much like an unreasonable child. Albeit that Oliver is older than me, I am his elder in all aspects except size and age. Responsibility for him fell on my shoulders from a young age after Dad had died and Mum had fallen into a deep spiral of depression. He became my shadow.

Oliver twists to look at me, but he just stands there, gazing through me, puzzled as if he was about to say something but can't recall what. His eyes light up when his thoughts return to him.

"Brad, why does the water only move that way?" he asks, referring to the small stream branching off the creek.

"I'm not sure, Oliver, I'm not sure." It is much more straightforward not to explain anything to Oliver that isn't important, as he ends up asking the same thing ten minutes later. I continue to stare at the stream, questioning my own thinking. Why *does* the water flow that way? I ask myself, but just as I begin to consider the thought, there is a sharp, crunching sound. Alarmed, I whip around to face the creek. Anticipating the worst, my eyes dart around, hoping Oliver has just thrown a rock into the shallows.

It was Oliver, but the sound was not that of a rock. It was Oliver's body tumbling down the bank, his limbs twisted like a rag doll, the pohutukawa saplings crushed by the path made by his heavy body. He lands facing away from me, so I cannot tell if his face is submerged underwater. I watch for a movement, listen for a sound. All I want to hear is one of Oliver's grunts, even just a childish cry, so I know that he is conscious. My body is paralyzed by what has just unfolded in front of me. The moment seems to linger. I want to leap down the bank to console Oliver but am unable to move.

Was that a giggle? The thought runs through my mind. I'm sure I heard a giggle, but he still isn't moving; he is lying in a lifeless state. Suddenly, my legs force my body to surge into the creek below, into the murky, diseased water splashing up my legs.

"Oliver! Oliver? Are you okay?"

A laugh. I hear Oliver chuckle. My wish has been answered, and now I know the giggle *was* Oliver. He hoists himself up out of the water, his arms straining against his weight. His large, glazed-over eyes meet mine, and he chuckles again.

"I trick'd ya Brad, I did, I trick'd ya." He leaps at me, his arms engulfing me as a child's would grasp his mother. We embrace each other, tumbling over because I can't hold him, and his weight plunges us both back into the creek. We giggle as we hold each other and Oliver squeals, overcome with delight that he had managed to trick me.

He squeezes me once more, and screams at the top of his lungs, "I trick'd ya Brad!"

CHARLOTTE BOYLE

Reconnaissance

My brother spent his childhood
fighting ninja octopus men
who crept up behind him
as he snuck down the hallway.

He learned to look both ways
before tiptoeing out of his bedroom.
But he never asked for my help.
He had a sabre
engraved with intricate swirls
it caught the light
as he battle-danced.
I watched him from my seat on the stairs.

Now he spends his days
six cities away
snarled up by loan sharks and taxes.
His weapon of choice is a volatile credit card
and no pleading of mine will convince him to change.
He says he never asked for my help.
My brother looks both ways
before crossing the street
as he tries to evade BMWs
and a receding hairline.

RUBY SOLLY

We All Fall Down

All those years
I thought that it was a pocket full of roses
but that night under the bridge
you taught me that it takes more than petals
to make kingdoms fall

It takes more than half a bag of pick and mix,
a pile of receipts and half a piece of shortbread
to survive a night
beside a fire that does not burn for you

You, brother
taught me many things
about how glamour is a state of mind
how water on fake fur becomes pearls
and how pinching your cheeks makes you
as beautiful as Marilyn
in the eyes of the slicked back boys

Back in the summer of pinky swears,
restricted licenses
and too much make-up
on too many girls' faces
Geisha girls and china dolls
itching for a minute in the spotlight
under the street lamp
beside your borrowed car

Back when you were master of the camera phone
with thousands upon thousands
of black and white blurs
a chess game melting
behind a liquid crystal display

To me you were not a boy
but a tropical bird
a misplaced creation of the gods
creating a hush and fall
wherever you went
filling in everyone's blanks
with the comforting stillness of blue
and the fiery depths of red

But seeing you tumble that night
falling fast from a childhood refuge
feet slipping over bricks and mortar
waiting patiently for the kings men to piece you together
I saw you only as our Southern Romeo
who gave so much away
that all he had left
was not enough

FRANCES BARNETT

Puddles

Each day after the clouds have let themselves go
I take you outside to look in the puddles.

Your brother and sister stay inside
too cold too wet too just–yuck –
they exclaim
but you come
bundled up in jacket and scarf
to see the new world.

It is a new world (says you)
you say that only when
the leaves have caught the droplets and the puddles
finally lie still and only then
when you look hard enough can you see
what really lies beneath the still sheets of water.

You say
with your face pressed to the ground
that water elephants live beneath them
and so do clowns
and there's ice-cream that never melts
and-and-and you say
its *perfect*.

As we walk back
I search for this other world in every reflection I see
I do not dream of
animals and clowns
but instead of a grown up you
who is still able to find the joy
in a puddle.

TRICIA NIEUWOUDT

Sepia Selfies

Here I am, milk-glass baby
in grandma's arms, she's
wearing a garden for a dress
white dog in her flower petal lap
glass bowl of chocolates on
shiny coffee table,
little jewels in
cellophane wrappers,
perfect
candy-bulbs

I can still feel my teeth
sugar-sting
and the toffee dribble
on my chin

And my mum
sun-smudged, pretty pink,
barely
tasting her 20s that
lemonade summer
just before uni

and it was
swimming pool, burnt lawn,
heat-soaked, cherry-coke normal
wet and mild water parks
Monet suburbia; everyone
photo album famous.

Nostalgia thickens feelings,
presses flowers flat, between swollen
album pages and
sepia selfies

they're warm soft proof
that I slept in that bed,
scraped my knees, peeled off
sun-bitten skin still
softly stinging

Photos are forever
Even though we're not

ADELAIDE PERRY

Shining Lantern, Smoky Car

When a man bikes but his
        dog
does not follow.

Leash stripped raw, pretty
pretty print corroded with deep cuts
from soiled claws and tooth marks
as smooth tail flickers swish
the air ripples with shocked waves and
        fibres
clawed from a plasma of urban lights and city heights
weaken the earth.
newspapers, like liquefaction, are no tell
all show.

When I was little
        tied land
was always orange.

I can remember the smell of stripped green hide
which hung off silver hooks in the window where you could watch
reddened ducks smile at the sight of twinkling knives.
Next door was there a doughnut shop
bright pink and sugared with circles
sprinkled with holes in yeast and teeth and parents' pockets
whose children would scream
for a sweet treat.

A time when
warm brown hands
would take me outside to be galvanised in gold.
She would pray for the present
        not knowing of the future

The smell of chrysanthemums
still lingers.

TRICIA NIEUWOUDT

Soaked in Light

Maybe we'll taste life
before it ruins us,
and leaves us
empty and divine,
our marble bodies,
shivering in the light
and maybe
I'll remember aching
with skin and pulse
like promises
and breath

and maybe, before decay,
and after we've sucked
the juice from our dreams,
gutted the world like
vampires with dripping mouths,
we'll live in a sunrise that
spills sky-dye from our bruised
teenage lips and

maybe you'll run
through a field of sun-haze,
like in those old movies
shot on film and soaked
in its own daylight and
maybe you'll cut yourself
on the edges of your soul
and lick the honeyed wound

and I'll taste my own halo,
feel it dribble down my chin
like plum juice and I'll wonder
if I could O.D. on my own light
or suffocate in such cruel brightness
as this flesh
and this life.

TIERNEY REARDON

For Auld Lang Syne

In a city that isn't ours
the times square ball will drop;
even further away, guns will fire
to ward off demons and darkness.

Our traditions seem just as strange;
we sing "auld lang syne"
without knowing the words
and drink to the new year
when we have no control over time.

In New Zealand we like to celebrate
under an open sky;
our year begins during a season
of peach trees and melted tar,
while our houses are still plagued
with tinsel and loud family members.

The night is filled with omens
if you can be bothered looking for them;
it's a superstitious time
for the most unlikely of people.
high priestesses and fools alike
fill their pockets with seeds,

and in quiet kitchen corners
fridge magnet poets
write their resolutions in the sugar
they spilled on the floor.

After the countdown,
fireworks punctuate seamless skies.

OLIVIA MAXWELL

No Salt on My Chips

There was no salt on my chips
in the Waihi dusk today. No salt on my chips,
and no refugees allowed onward to Germany.

Me in my jacket that probably cost more than a train ticket,
with cheeks tinged pink from the cold;
tossing scraps of fish to seagulls
and laughing at their strange, long-legged shadows
in the setting sun.

Me, watching the same sleepy sun
that somewhere is waking up to
the stale, sweaty, desperate smell
of a thousand people who slept in a train station last night.

Sometimes it's hard to remember
that the far side of the world is a real place
not some vaguely remembered childhood story
with a moral at the end: the fox and the crow,
the hare and the tortoise, the man and the war.

And when the Arab Spring seems more distant,
less known and less tangible
than the taste of soggy chips and tomato sauce,
I find that all those troubled souls on the six o'clock news
melt into an endless parade of background characters,
those one-dimensional caricatures
only worth a single word biography:
the butcher, the baker, the refugee waiting in Budapest;
and they drift in and out on the sea breeze
like background characters always do,
before anyone really stops to look.

A train station full of normal clothes and normal names,
that's what I know I'd see
but still can't quite manage to imagine;
people who were teachers and doctors and all sorts back home,
who were proud when their children learnt to talk,
and who cried when their grandparents died.
People who probably also laugh at seagulls,
people who have once known and will again
know no worry greater than
the lack of salt on their own dinner.

FREDDIE CORMACK-SMITH

The Bard's Last Song

Nathaniel had seen paper only once before, through the latticed window of a manor house. A boy had sat in a chair, frowning in deep befuddlement at the thin, flaky object. A clear, jagged tear fell from the young one's eye. He howled and flung the page across the room.

Holding the brick made of leather and tree bark, Nathaniel could now see why. The lines twisted and writhed as if they were demons dancing a wild, frenzied ritual to some dark entity. It was when he saw the picture of a scrawny boy being bathed in light, holding a sword high above his head, that he realized what the lines meant.

Nathaniel dropped the book and walked away. Away from the regal messengers of the lords, away from the hearty laughter of townsfolk shaking with mirth at the brightly clad jesters, and away from the small, squat huts of hardworking peasants.

Deaf to the striking of the blacksmith's anvil, deaf to the clop of horses' hooves on the windswept moors, and deaf even to the requests from strangers for him to sing, he walked the dirt road.

His lute bumped against a wall bordering him from farmland. As it struck, a single string quivered. A note of pure perfection shattered the silence. Nathaniel looked upon it the way a hero looks on his lover, all trials aside. He picked it up and began to strum and sing with ecstasy.

He played every song and every story he knew. Every one for the last time.

LYDIA WHYTE

The Sandpaper Effect

I'm not sure how. Especially after the life he'd lived in India with his wife and kids. I always remember Mum had thought they were really rich, because his wife used Elizabeth Arden cosmetics in the bleak, post-war '40s. The wife died, the kids drifted away; and one way or another, he can't have had much money left. No more *ayahs*.

So anyway, by 1980, when Mum and I returned to England, it was a bit of a surprise that he was living at Nan's. Sleeping on a fold-out couch. With us visiting, it was truly cramped. Four of us packed in like canned pilchards: Nan, Great Uncle Jock, Mum and me. A tiny, one-bedroom council flat is not designed to house a large elderly woman and a washed-up war veteran; let alone a fourteen year old and her mother.

Pristine Jock wore a collar and tie even though he spent his days on the couch. That I remember. And he loved the cricket. Though cordial, conversation was fairly limited at first, because he was such a quiet man. Tiny, too. Here was I at five foot ten, and there was Jock at five foot nothing. He had a crinkly but kind face, topped by a shiny bald head with just a smudge of white hair around the sides. The gold-frame glasses perched on the bridge of his nose always looked vaguely precarious.

For some reason Jock took quite a shine to me. Being a teenager who was inquisitive, I think I surprised him. I'd not met him before, or if I had, couldn't remember it. He was the older half-brother of my Granddad, who had died when I was nine. I'd loved him dearly and still felt his loss. Jock seemed like a window into something I longed to see again. And so, each morning, I made a point of sitting down and having a chat with him. Quietly, he enjoyed an audience and I loved hearing what he had to say. And once he opened up, boy, did he have something to say.

By the end of our first week I couldn't stop him talking. Whenever I sat down, he'd pick up his story exactly where he'd left off the day before. It seemed a feverish compulsion to unburden his experiences. Nan later told Mum that he'd never said anything about the war to anyone else; her included.

I loved every second of it. And he was quite graphic, in view of my age. I respected that about him, too. I just wish I could remember more of what he said. Couple of days ago, trying to pin down details, I dug out my old diary. To my shame, I recorded fully what we ate at just about every meal; but there were only hints of the nuggets he shared with me. "Today we talked about Passchendaele."

That story is inscribed in my mind. It wasn't his first battle. He'd been at the Somme, too. But at Passchendaele Jock's mate got a bullet in the brain. Right next to him. Literally splattered with it. He told me that wasn't the worst bit, though. He'd just kept moving. Left the boy lying there, face obliterated. I don't think he processed what had happened until later; it was just self-preservation kicking in. That's all that kept him moving.

Weird thing is that he'd tell me a story like that one day, and then for the next few days he'd talk about the boredom that went with war. The hanging around and endless waiting for the next bit of action. Maybe this is how men coped: focusing on the irritations. From what Jock said, there were plenty.

Lice. Now they really got to him. He was constantly scratching. The soldiers would hold candles near the seams of their clothing, because that was where the lice laid their eggs. The candle's heat would make the eggs explode. Of course, miss one and you'd be off scratching again. Even if someone else missed one, you would eventually end up scratching. He said when he got leave and went home, his stepmother would make him take a bath outside because she didn't want vermin in the house. And then, she'd boil or burn his uniform. Jock said it was bliss to wear something clean, too. Probably why he was fastidious till the day he died.

And there were rats. "Rats the size of cats," he said. To be honest, I thought he was exaggerating; and it wasn't till I was at university writing an essay about life in the trenches that I remembered his words. The rats were huge because they feasted on dead bodies. There was a plentiful supply.

"Do you know what a tin whistle sounds like?" he asked me one morning. For him, the sound meant death. A sergeant would blow this kind of whistle before they went "over the top". As soon as they vacated the trenches, men would be scythed down like blades of grass. Cut off at the knees. Telling me that, was the only time he cried. The shrill of a whistle struck terror in his heart. It put him off football because the sound still reverberated in his head. "Fear is a terrible thing, my dear. Facing your fears isn't much fun, either." I held his hand that day.

At one point he was stationed near a little French village. I can't tell you the name of it. Of course all the men from the village were away fighting for France, so the women developed an industry around catering for the nearby soldiers. I assumed, in a very worldly way, that he was talking about prostitution; but he said that while some men did seek "female comfort" the really thriving business was laundry. Recounting the simple bliss of getting something clean and lice-free back from those "wonderful women" lit his face up with delight. The other real treat was home-cooked egg and chips.

The first time he went to Paris he was on leave. He didn't focus much on that, though. I suppose any joy of such a time is bound to be over-shadowed by the hulking war. He simply said: "On that occasion, I drank too much."

At Passchendaele Jock was shot in the thigh, "just a flesh wound." His only companion at the time was a young British soldier whose stomach wound was far worse. They were in a shell crater. And Jock was, literally, stuck in the mud. When the hole started to fill with water, Jock's injured leg was trapped, and the young soldier was lying face-down. The boy drowned. Right in front of him. His eyes had pleaded for help, but Jock was stuck and the kid was yards away. He'd leant forward holding his gun out for the boy to grab, but neither could reach the other. Repeatedly, he muttered, "the noise was terrible": the gurgling and the sucking sound of the mud as he tried to free his leg. He sat with his eyes shut for a long time after telling me that. I wondered if we'd come to the end of the road. But he had some dogged determination to get everything off his chest. My role was to help alleviate the pain.

In another shell hole he met a German officer. I'm not sure which battle. Jock jumped in for cover, and the German was already there, with a terrible leg wound. They sat there pointing their guns at each other until, eventually, they put them down. Helmut's thigh was bleeding badly and Jock took off his belt to make a tourniquet for him. Helmut, an older, educated man, spoke English. They talked. Helmut showed Jock a photo of his beautiful blonde wife and daughter. It was funny to hear him talk about this man as a person, and not just "the Boche" or "the Huns". Eventually, Jock crawled out of the hole and back across No Man's Land. As he left, Helmut said, quite formally, something along the lines of "it is heartening to see, that even in such horror as this, humanity does not abandon us completely." Jock still wondered whether Helmut survived. "In another life we might have been friends." It was in this story that I asked a rare question: "Why didn't you kill him? He was the enemy." Jock shook his head at me. "I never wanted to kill anyone." I knew then that the subject was taboo.

You know, I wish I'd listened better. Or used a tape recorder. Memory fails me. Jock told me other jaw-dropping stories, and I simply can't remember them. He would shut his eyes as he talked, the movie of his war playing in a never-ending loop. He never spoke about "the Great War", as he called it, to anyone before me or after. Sixty years of silence. It felt odd to associate the horror of these experiences with the little man in front of me. Because, despite all that he had endured, he loved cricket, had a family, lived in India and wore his collar and tie. I feel as though I can't do his stories justice. Like used sandpaper, time has worn away.

He died the following year. They buried him on the morning of Prince Charles and Lady Diana's wedding. He couldn't stand fireworks. Nan said he always went "jittery".

FINN SHAW

Sonnet IV – The Wheel

Umber, Lannister, Tully and Martell;
Tyrell, Targaryen, Arryn and Stark.
They're spokes on the wheel, and all is not well,
winning a war is no walk in the park.

The Stags of the South have fallen from grace,
whilst something moves from the East and the North.
The survivors pounce to claim the top place,
at court, the villains and traitors come forth.

But Summer is failing, Winter is coming;
and soon the longest of all nights shall fall.
Westeros of old has come to nothing,
when they're in great need who'll answer the call?

A princess has servants and fighters who kneel,
but can she, or will she destroy the wheel?

ELLIOTT HUGHES

Hurtgen Forest

19 September to 16 December 1944

The forest waltzed in the moonlight
and all through the day
trees swayed in sombre steps
to drumbeats that rolled across a tormented sky.

Men danced in groups,
clawing and stabbing,
their silver fish whining among the trees.

Day deepened into dusk
and still the men danced,
leaving many slumped behind.

Reverse lightning leapt into the sky.
Sudden mushrooms of earth rose
and arced downwards.

The hoof beats of the Second Rider tore across the night.

Dawn came again
files of soldiers staggered
drunk on death.

They came again,
turned over the earth,
marked the ground with pale white crosses.

The guns moved north-east.

MICAELA MEDER

Writing Hand

She has always been too sensitive, she knows. With her face apparently an open book and her imagination all too wild, she is altogether too soft in a hard world.

"You feel too deeply, dear, and it'll only hurt you in the end," they would often warn her. At first she had laughed; it had never been a secret to her, after all. Still, to this day, she just doesn't know how to stop *feeling*. She seems to absorb all kinds of energy and emotions that she encounters in daily life—negative as well as positive.

She used to have the hope that, while it may be her greatest weakness, it might one day prove to be her greatest strength. So, over the years she has learnt to cope: she writes. And writes and writes. When her mind becomes too full, her heart too heavy with the emotional output of family, friends, fictional characters, the world ... her writing hand sets to work. If it didn't, she would have long since found her *self* buried under it all. Nestled in the palm of her writing hand lies her sanity. Even though her heart would be carried by the paper—open for all to see—at least it would no longer be trapped. What else do you do when there is just too much inside of you?

Too much, too much, too ...

It was almost Anzac Day. Well beforehand, she had mentally prepared herself. A huge part of the purpose of the commemorative day is to encourage people to acknowledge the tragic reality of the war ... but she had never needed to be persuaded. The soldiers *deserve* to be remembered—and her imagination had already pictured the war in painful detail. So she tried not to get too emotionally involved, tried to remember the soldiers' sacrifices without thinking on what exactly the sacrifices entailed. This was nigh impossible. And even harder when the day came that she stood where they had stood one hundred years ago.

Visiting war cemeteries on the Gallipoli Peninsula was eye-opening and exhausting. But the soldiers deserved to be visited where they had fallen, so far from home. A weight of sorrow had settled on her shoulders and it grew heavier with every gravestone she saw. There were too many. It was ... too heavy.

But how much heavier had the weight been on the shoulders of those courageous men?

She knelt beside a grave and traced the name carved on the headstone. The stone grazed her fingers but she felt no pain, for the biting cold had already numbed them. Her breath clouded the frigid air, and for a brief moment she could have sworn that she saw the face of a young man in it before the likeness evaporated. She shook the notion off. It was obvious that her writer's imagination had simply taken her hostage again.

As the day wore on, she sometimes thought she saw figures in her peripheral vision, but when she turned her head no one was there. It wouldn't have bothered her so much if it weren't for the fact that they always seemed to be in military uniform.

She couldn't wait to leave the Peninsula. But the ghosts travelled across the water and returned to visit her at night. She would dream of death and a red sky. Waking up severely shaken, a teary mess, she desperately tried to convince herself that the nightmare had simply been the result of an overly upsetting day combined with her overactive imagination.

Little did she know that things would only get much worse. Every night, there were different soldiers—and different deaths, but the same dying moments. Every day she could feel a little of herself die alongside her soldiers. Sometimes, in the moment that her eyes whipped open after a nightmare, she'd see her soldiers standing sentry around her room. Then, within the blink of an eye, they'd disappear. Without a sound.

Tonight, they'll be back. Her writing hand twitches—rather like the flutter of a bird's broken wing.

How can you write of what has consumed you when it has become *you? The soldiers' story has become her story, and her story has become theirs.*

And so she sits here now, reliving it all with trembling ink as she pens her nightmares on torn and crumpled paper. It has become her duty to write. Her blessing, her curse, her escape, her passion. She was born to write the stories that were just too *hard* to be told out loud. Surely the future can't mean the death of the past—not when it continues to live on in people like her?

The stories fight her writing hand even as they become infused with the ink that stains memories to the page. They fight so hard that panic starts to bubble up in her chest as she struggles to set her mind free, her hand steadily weakening under the onslaught of the devastating images that it has to translate into words.

The past is a heavy thing to carry into the future. Were shoulders built to bear such weight? It hurts. *The soldiers had hurt. Her soldiers had hurt. In the confines of her mind they continue to hurt. Hurt her mind. Hurt her heart. Hurt-hurt-hurt. How can a person die hundreds of deaths in a day and still live to sleep through hundreds more before dawn? It's still too much, still too much, too much, too much…*

"You feel too deeply, dear…"
TOO MUCH!
"… and it'll only hurt you in the end."

Her writing hand shudders and falls limp.

TIERNEY REARDON

Trapping Moths

Before you get it into your head that she belongs to you or that she will change for you, take another look at her. Look how straight her back is; that posture comes from not quite two decades of bowing to nobody. Curiously, she is not reading or listening to the radio; she is content to just sit and look out of the bus window as street lights pass in blurs. Her breath fogs up the glass, turns the lights to orange-gold suns.

Sometimes she will go without washing her hair for days; on these days the words come to her faster than thoughts, threaten to trip her up. She can't control them any more than you can. Living off cups of tea and instant noodles, she channels this delicate catharsis of hers onto paper. Trapping words like moths, pinning their wings down. She always looks for her horoscope in the bookstores. You're not meant to read magazines before buying them, which makes her wonder if fortunes must be earned before they come true.

Capturing moths will not pay for the tea and noodles, let alone fortunes. She spends hours at a time behind a checkout, scanning cans of beans and picking pieces of change from the cash register. It's easy enough to slip into a rhythm: scanning, bagging, printing receipts, over and over until the sky outside darkens to indigo. The collective sound of a hundred squeaking trolley wheels, and plastic bags being shaken open, is enough to make time stand still.

Weekends are the best days. She folds her time into origami stars; they collect in piles on her desk, in cupboards, under her bed. The words gather in her mind like thunderclouds, then all at once the storm will begin. Lightning threatens to set her notebooks alight. Rejection letters collect in her mailbox, but so do letters of acceptance, of good news. After all, a story does no good if you keep it to yourself. Even so, there is an exercise book on a shelf where she keeps the poems that belong to her alone.

You don't know this. You only see her bright eyes, hair dyed red from the roots to the split ends, her boots, her cardigan covered in fluff. You see her bracelets, chipped nail polish, the makeup that has almost worn off her eyes. Like a poem, you can even see the smudges of ink on her fingertips. You don't know anything else though, so don't think for a second that she belongs to you. Don't you dare think that she might change for you. She has moths to trap, tea to drink, storms to create. She does not have the time to have her heart broken by you. So look again, look down, look away. She won't be yours.

JOSIE BERLINER

An Ode to Procrastination

Why, tell why, do you seize my pen
nail down my blankets
punch snooze again and again
and glue down my eyelids
against the morning sun?

Oh, sticky fingered procrastination
slipping a shadow over the clock
locking the front door
hiding the key
maybe a sick day would be best?

An ode to you, procrastination
slippery, slimy being
that shoots jelly into my thoughts
half-set
that with time will turn to hardened resolve
but at this moment
could be melted with ease.

I swear an oath
to strike thee dead
but maybe next week–
I'd rather stay in bed.

Guidance for applicants

You've written your story, arrived at a final version. Printed out, it looks OK on the page. You send it off. That's it?

Well, not necessarily. Is it honestly the very BEST work you can present? Did you really take full notice of the entry guidelines, or just skim over them and hope for the best?

The purpose of good presentation of any written work—be it online, on paper, a professional report, a job application, a magazine article—is to make it as easy as possible for the reader to read, understand and enjoy, *first time round*. For *Re-Draft*, you face two pretty tough judges who need to be convinced your story has earned its place.

Yes, we think the standard is higher than it was five years ago, so full marks for that, teachers and students.

But here are some things that put the judges off right at the start:

- Text presented in tiny 8pt font, giving the judges eyestrain
- Pictures or watermarks behind text—a no-no
- Long long rambling paragraphs—hard to read, horrible if in 8 pt font
- Stories or poems centre-justified; other fancy layouts or fonts.

And here are some things that will give your story the best possible chance:

- Titles as headers at top of page; but no author names on MS
- 12pt Times Roman, one side of page only (this is industry MS standard)
- Good logical paragraphing, especially of dialogue
- Proper punctuation (learn the difference between it's *vs* its, and know that its' is a nonsense)
- Evidence of good self-editing.

Lastly, here's a technique writers like Joy Cowley use and strongly recommend.

Finish your story, put it away for a few days. Come back to it, not as "the writer," but as a *reader*. Not two days before the deadline, but say, two weeks before, or preferably longer. Try to read it as if for the first time. Read it out aloud.

And then do a final edit. Be really hard about those fussy overdone adjectives and adverbs, the unnecessary explanations, the *showing* (through action) and not *telling* (describing feelings). Find the best, most punchy verbs, which are one of the glories of the English language.

You'll probably surprise yourself, how much better you can still make your story. And send it off knowing it's the best you can do.

2016 Checklist for Entrants

Complete this checklist before sending your entries.
It is for your own benefit. There is no need to send the checklist to us.

☐ You must be aged 13–19 years at the time of entering.

☐ If you are entering for the first time and are no longer at school, provide proof of age.

☐ Send your own original work typed in Times Roman, on white A4 paper, one side only.

☐ DO NOT send work that has already been published, submitted for publication elsewhere (including the internet) or entered for another competition. (School magazines excepted.)

☐ Send TWO COPIES of each entry. Maximum three entries allowed per person. We prefer that you send your work unfolded, in an A4 sized envelope.

☐ There is no word limit but entries must be suitable for publication in an anthology.

☐ Polish (redraft, punctuate and proofread) your work before sending. There is no need for fancy fonts and arty layouts. The judges will be more impressed by careful paragraphing and punctuation!

☐ DO NOT write your name on your work.

☐ DO write the title of your work at the top of the first page. DO NOT include footers or headers e.g. Google documents.

☐ CLEARLY write your name and the other information requested on the 2016 Entry Form and enclose ONE COPY of this with your entries.

☐ POST your entries to Re-Draft Competition
P.O. Box 21120
Christchurch 8143

Deadline for entries is 30 September 2016.

Other information you need

▸ Entries are acknowledged on receipt and results will be advised by post.

▸ Results will be available in November 2016.

▸ The judges' decision is final. No correspondence will be entered into.

▸ The editors of the collection reserve the right to make minor editorial changes to your work, without consultation. You will be sent a copy of your edited work for approval.

▸ Each successful entrant receives a free copy of the 2016 book. All entrants may purchase copies at prices well below the retail price set for the book.

2016 Re-Draft Entry Form

Send ONE COPY of this form with your entries.
Use the checklist on the opposite page before sending your work.
Please write clearly!

Contributor's name ....

Postal address you will be at in November ....

.... Post Code ....

(street address or box number, town, city or other location)

Telephone (land line essential) .... cell phone (optional) ....

Email address ....

Date of birth .... / .... / .... ☐ Student ☐ or Occupation: ....

Name of your school, university, polytechnic or other ....

.... Year level ....

Principal's name (school students only) ....

Head of English (school students only) ....

Creative writing teacher ....

Don't forget to send TWO copies of each entry.

Titles of entries (1) ....

(2) ....

(3) ....

CHECK: Is your name on your work? If it is, please take it off.

(This does not mean that you need to remove the titles from your entries.)

Declaration

These entries are my own original work. They have not already been published or submitted for publication elsewhere and are not entered for other competitions. Nor will they be published, submitted or entered elsewhere until the results of this Re-Draft competition are known.

I give permission for the School for Young Writers to edit and publish my work and to use part or whole of it to promote the competition and the resulting publication.

Signature .... Date ....

POST your entries to: Re-Draft Competition
PO Box 21120
Christchurch 8143

DEADLINE
FOR ENTRIES :
30 SEPTEMBER 2016

THE EDITOR: We can't have much more of this, space must also be found
for my stuff.

MYSELF: All right, never hesitate to say so. I can turn off the tap at will.

*Flann O'Brien (*The Best of Myles, *1968)*

Index of Contributors

Eleanor Loader	1st year, University of East Anglia, UK	24, 39
Mary Locker	Year 10, Logan Park High School, Dunedin	129
Rose McCulloch	Year 13, Kaikorai Valley College, Dunedin	43
Gemma McLeod	Freelance writer, Auckland	67
Duncan Matchett*	Year 12, Cashmere High School, Christchurch	60, 130
Olivia Maxwell	1st year, University of Auckland	73, 106, 139
Micaela Meder	1st year, University of Auckland	145
Ana Menzies	Year 12, Wellington High School	64
Niki Menzies	Year 12, Wellington High School	120
Ala'h Musa	Year 13, Whangarei Girls' High School	56
Tricia Nieuwoudt	Year 13, Palmerston North Girls' High School	135, 137
Catherine Norman	Year 11, Palmerston North Girls' High School	18
Alice Park	Year 9, Macleans College, Auckland	71, 116
Jake Parsons*	Year 12, St Andrew's College, Christchurch	53
Adelaide Perry*	Year 11, St Margaret's College, Christchurch	2, 50, 136
Sam Poles Smith	Year 11, Francis Douglas Memorial College, New Plymouth	131
Emma Rattenbury	Year 13, New Plymouth Girls' High School	117
Pru Rhynd	Year 12, Whangarei Girls' High School	84
Tierney Reardon*	Year 11, homeschooled, Christchurch	87, 138, 147
Finn Shaw	Year 12, Tauranga Boys' College	143
Caroline Shepherd	Year 11, Epsom Girls' Grammar School, Auckland	101
Ruby Solly	2nd year, Victoria University of Wellington	41, 80, 133
Cian Sutherland	Year 10, Hamilton Boys' High School	12
Mia Sutherland*	Year 9, Cashmere High School, Christchurch	114
Joel Tauafao-Anae	Year 11, Melville High School, Hamilton	72
Monique Thorp	1st year, Victoria University of Wellington	13, 31, 115
Jacinta van der Linden	Year 11, Kaitaia College	127
Lara Watson*	Year 13, Gisborne Girls' High School	85, 93
Bridget White*	Year 13, Christchurch Girls' High School	99
Lydia Whyte*	Year 10, Nga Tawa Diocesan School, Marton	141
Charlotte Williams*	Year 10, Palmerston North Girls' High School	3, 51
Petra Williamson*	Year 13, Christchurch Girls' High School	102
Hayley Xie	Year 9, Macleans College, Auckland	130

* Denotes current or past School for Young Writers student